It's Not Over is a gripping story of hope when circum-stances seem dark. Ricardo Sanchez has beautifully written a book that is an uplifting source of inspira-tion for anyone. The insights are full of wisdom! If you are in a difficult season or life is good, I highly recom-mend this book.

—DAN REILAND
EXECUTIVE PASTOR, 12STONE CHURCH

Ricardo Sanchez has been my close true friend for twenty years. His heart for God and for people, both believers and unbelievers, is unparalleled. This book and its powerful message both honor God and strengthen human hearts.

The underscore is such a crucial theme for the chal-lenging days we currently live in. It will no doubt encourage and challenge your soul to never give up on our limitless God.

—ISRAEL HOUGHTON
INTERNATIONAL WORSHIP LEADER AND CHRISTIAN
RECORDING ARTIST
GRAMMY, DOVE, STELLAR AWARD WINNER

The best music in our world normally comes out of people who have walked the journey they sing about. Ricardo's book, *It's Not Over*, is a testament to who he knows our God to *be*. Like Ricardo's music, this book will bless you. When we "fall and fail" as Christians, it's not over because of our attachment to Jesus. That refrain needs to run through our spiritual DNA! If you are overcoming anything or know somebody who is, this book is for you and for them. I pray this book reaches our world in a powerful way.

—Carl Lentz
Pastor, Hillsong NYC

What an inspirational story that the Sanchez family shares with us! It's such a reminder of God's grace and goodness. Ricardo's music has been an encouragement to me for so long, and now his family's story has lifted me up even more. I am reminded that when it comes to God's miracles…it's not over!

—Mac Powell
Lead Singer, Third Day

Ricardo Sanchez has written an amazing book that offers a hope-hungry world exactly what it's starving for. In his new book Ricardo takes us on his own personal journey from intense battle to incredible breakthrough. He inspires us to remember, that even in our darkest days, we must not give up; we must look up. Because when we do, we'll discover, just as he did, that no matter what it looks like, it's not over.

—Jim Raley
Senior Pastor, Calvary Christian Center
Ormond Beach, Florida, and Orlando, Florida

Ricardo Sanchez epitomizes what a worship leader should be. As a man that has made a lifetime out of encouraging others, teaching faith and worship, Ricardo had his own faith tested through near tragedy. *It's Not Over* will encourage everyone who reads or hears of this story. Through biblical examples of faith,

Ricardo shows how he and his family were victorious and provides excellent insight into how we can also win when life's challenges face us.

—Richie Hughes
Speaker, Author of *Start Here, Go Anywhere*

it's **NOT OVER**

it's NOT OVER

RICARDO SANCHEZ

PASSIO

Most CHARISMA HOUSE BOOK GROUP products are available at special quantity discounts for bulk purchase for sales promotions, premiums, fund-raising, and educational needs. For details, write Charisma House Book Group, 600 Rinehart Road, Lake Mary, Florida 32746, or telephone (407) 333-0600.

IT's NOT OVER by Ricardo Sanchez
Published by Passio
Charisma Media/Charisma House Book Group
600 Rinehart Road
Lake Mary, Florida 32746
www.charismahouse.com

Cover design by Justin Evans
Design Director: Bill Johnson

Visit the author's website at www.ricardomusic.com.

Library of Congress Control Number: 2012909940
International Standard Book Number: 978-1-61638-833-1
E-book ISBN: 978-1-61638-834-8

While the author has made every effort to provide accurate telephone numbers and Internet addresses at the time of publication, neither the publisher nor the author assumes any responsibility for errors or for changes that occur after publication.

First edition

12 13 14 15 16 — 9 8 7 6 5 4 3 2 1
Printed in the United States of America

*This book is dedicated to my wife,
Jennette, and our three sons,
Ricardo, Josiah, and Micah.
I love you. It's not over.*

CONTENTS

FOREWORD

THE LIFE OF believer is not about the absence of struggle; it is about success through struggle. We are told that because of what Christ has done, we are "more than conquerors." It is a very simple truth that the only way to be classified as a conqueror is to embrace the challenge of conflict. In Revelation we are told that we overcome by the blood of the Lamb and the word of our testimony. The word of your testimony is the spoken declaration of the triumph that Christ bought for you with His shed blood that you would never have known had it not been for the grace and mercy of God.

Conflict and struggle come in every shape, form, and fashion, and at times can suddenly shatter the life that you live. I want you to be encouraged by the word of the testimony locked in the pages of this book by Ricardo Sanchez, *It's Not Over*. It is a powerful reminder that while things here on the earth can seem to change in an instant, nothing in heaven changes. God still sits on His throne, He is still all powerful, and He can still move heaven and earth to bring you through your conflict as more than a conqueror.

Is it going to be tough? Absolutely, but it's not over!

Is it going change you? Without a doubt, but it's not over!

Are you going to make it? With God all things are possible;

if you have breath in your lungs and can see the sun in the sky, you have a reason to shout with the voice of triumph, "It's not over" and keep marching to your victory!

Press on, child of God; the Master is not through with you yet! It's not over!

—MATTHEW HAGEE
EXECUTIVE PASTOR, CORNERSTONE CHURCH
SAN ANTONIO, TEXAS

1

THE PRESSING OF LIFE

*"I need Thee, O I need Thee. Every
hour I need Thee..."*[1]

PLEASE PUT ALL tray tables and seat backs in their
full and upright position." The flight attendants
were preparing the cabin for landing. As a traveling
minister and musician, I've done the flying routine countless
times. Making our final descent into Jacksonville, Florida,
was the beginning stop on a several-weeks-long ministry trip.
Florida was a short flight from Atlanta, and I had just kissed
my boys good-bye and enjoyed a nice drive to the airport with
my wife. Jennette enjoys occasionally driving me to the airport,
and I enjoy having her drive with me. It often provides a few
minutes together in the midst of our busy life.

As my plane touched down in Jacksonville, I began to

gather my belongings and reach for my cell phone, as was my normal procedure upon approaching the runway. The pilot touched down, and I powered on my phone while the plane began to taxi toward the gate. What happened next was surreal and hit me like a ton of bricks. Immediately when my phone powered up, texts began to flash on my screen: "911—CALL HOME," "URGENT—CALL ME," "Josiah has been hurt—call ASAP." My head began to spin as I was bombarded with desperate texts and phone messages. The voice mail from Jennette still rings in my head today: "Josiah is being life-flighted to Scottish Rite Children's Hospital. The doctors are saying the worst. Please call." Her message was calm but interrupted with weeping. I felt as though someone had punched me in the gut. "What? Why? How could this be happening to my son? This has to be a horrible nightmare. What possibly could have happened?"

Have you ever noticed life has a way of throwing you curveballs when you least expect it? If you've lived long enough, I'm sure you've had a few experiences of your own where you weren't sure how all the pieces were going to fit together and how the brokenness would all make sense. Paul refers to running the "race of life" in 1 Corinthians 9:24. The Message Bible says the words "run to win."

How do you *run to win* when you feel the very *wind* has been knocked out of you? How do you find the endurance to finish when the pain seems overbearing? Maybe you've watched a spouse walk out on you. Maybe you've lost your life savings in the faltering economy. Maybe you've received a tragic report from your doctor. Maybe you're watching your children make decisions that are pushing them from the things of God. Whatever it is, if you've lived life, you've experienced pain. You've experienced what I call "the pressing"—those moments when you proclaim in faith, "It's not over," though everything in the natural may look and feel exactly the opposite. This was most certainly one of those moments for my family and me.

Though oftentimes could be confused as "de-pressing," I believe this season I refer to as "the pressing" can be a strength and step of victory if you extract the life principles my wife and I recently had to walk through with our nine-year-old son, Josiah. You are called to be an overcomer and walk a victorious life, but sometimes the practicality of walking victoriously in the midst of pressure can feel overbearing.

My hope is, as you read this book, you will learn to harvest strength, build faith and confidence, and complete your journeys with joy, trust, and a strong testimony to share with the world around you. I believe the prophetic voice for this generation is the message of "it's not over," the message that even though things might look dismal, God is still on the throne and wants to be involved in your situation. The Bible says in Isaiah 59:19, "When the enemy shall come in like a flood, the Spirit of the Lord shall lift up a standard against him" (KJV). Whatever your season may look like right now, remember it's just a season and God can turn it around.

ALLOW THE PRESS TO EMPOWER

As a young boy growing up, my father was a command sergeant major in the United States Army. It was imperative that his uniform looked immaculate at all times. I'll never forget watching my mother prepare his clothes for him. She would take a pass over his shirt with her hot iron. Again and again the hot iron would roll over and over the shirt until all the wrinkles were "pressed" out. I think life has a way of "pressing" on us. The Bible says, "We are pressed on every side by troubles, but we are not crushed" (2 Cor. 4:8, NLT). Oftentimes in the midst of the pressing, the heat and the pressures of life sometimes feel overbearing as if you can no longer take the weight of the burdens. But if you surrender to the process of being pressed, I believe you will come out at the end just like my father's shirts—wrinkle-free! There's a perfecting and an empowering that can occur during "the pressing."

Walking off the plane that horrible day, I remember feeling as if something had just sucked all the life from me. I quickly returned the 911-calls I had received, and I came to learn that Josiah was at a friend's house swimming in their pool with his older brother, Ricardo II, and several other children. The boys were playing, as boys do, and doing tricks into the shallow end of the friend's pool.

Josiah is a lover of life. He enjoys laughing, but he *really* enjoys getting people to laugh. All the kids were doing stunts, each attempting to outdo the previous boy's effort. In an attempt to get the biggest laugh, Josiah decided to dive, hands at his side, through an inflatable pool ring in the shallow end of a swimming pool. Underestimating the pool depth, Josiah dove and took direct impact to his head, causing a complete loss of feeling in his body. Josiah was pulled to the pool deck, crying out in pain and in fear. He knew something was seriously wrong.

Here I was sitting in an airport hundreds of miles away from my family...hundreds of miles away from Josiah, feeling completely inadequate and unable to help. Honestly I felt like I wanted to punch something. I was upset and angry and confused all at once. As a man I wanted to cover and protect my family. It brings a sense of honor. But there was nothing I could do at that present time while sitting in the airport. I couldn't be with my wife as she had to watch the helicopter fly off with our son. I couldn't be with Josiah as he was alone with the paramedics hearing words such as, "He'll never walk again." I couldn't touch and hug my baby or my other sons through the phone line. So many thoughts went through my head: "God, I'm here serving You, and this is what happens? Where are You, God? Why weren't You there to protect Josiah?"

I'd like to tell you how heroic I was in my faith and how as a man of God I immediately took control of the situation, but it simply wasn't the case. I had taken a blow right where it hurt the most. Something had happened to one of my babies. All of the natural signs and reports coming in were shouting that my son's life was over. I've experienced some pressing in my life, but nothing compares to dealing with an injury or loss to one of your children. I was somehow wishing I could take the place of my son and bear the pain he was going through.

DON'T ALLOW THE PRESSING TO BE PARALYZING

My family shared an experience several months prior to this event with Josiah that triggered a similar physical reaction for me as I was trying to process the reports I was receiving about my son. The past summer our family had spent some time off the central coast of California. We intentionally were trying to harvest every opportunity to make memories with our sons and find new adventures on every trip. With that spirit in mind we decided to take a canoeing trip off the coastline, hoping to find a much-talked-about infamous local's spot with underwater caves that were known to have incredible sea life and beauty.

The only day we had to take the trip was a bit windy and a little choppy on the sea. Additionally, the water temperature was only in the low fifties. The ideal conditions would have been completely still, no waves and no wind. But we were determined to be adventurous and conquer our quest to find these caves. In order to get out into the ocean, we first had to vigorously row beyond the breaking waves, which appeared to grow in fierceness and height as we watched. I was partnered with my oldest son, Ricardo. Neither of us had ever canoed before, much less out in the ocean. We had to time our entry into the water perfectly in between each breaking wave. We had to be synchronized, focused, and quick. The canoe had to be pointed straight into the face of the oncoming ocean. Any angle would flip our boat.

The first wave came, and we successfully made it through. Victory! Wave after wave was crashing against our canoe. Now about fifty yards out into the ocean, we had tackled most of the boat-flipping waves. As my son began to notice how far offshore we had come and how close we were to sea otters and sea life swimming around us, the fear that we could easily be *in* the water began to overpower his strength to stay focused. The next wave that came took our boat over with it.

The fifty-three-degree water immediately hit my chest, sucking every breath out as a vapor. The icy chill made every movement more intense and more painful. A thousand things were going through my head. At six feet, five inches, I still couldn't touch the bottom of the ocean. I was way beyond the kelp bed that served as the barrier for sharks. My son was stuck under the canoe. Waves were hitting us, and I literally couldn't breath because the water was so cold. I felt like Leonardo DiCaprio in the closing scenes of the *Titanic* when he was stuck in the iceberg-laden water, struggling for every breath to communicate. The fact was, we had lost our balance. A wave flipped our world upside down, and my ability to recover was limited by my conditions. That's the exact picture the enemy wants to put in your head when you encounter a "pressing" in life. But you can't allow the pressing to be paralyzing.

Now here I am sitting in terminal A in the Jacksonville airport just waiting for a way to get to my son, feeling like I did when I tipped into the icy ocean, but this time I'm not in the water. Literally, I felt as if something were hindering my breathing, almost as if something heavy was sitting on my chest. So heavy, in fact, even speaking was laborious. Something had flipped my boat, but this time it wasn't literal. This time I had no control. This time I couldn't see the wave coming. This time there was no instruction course on how to get back into the canoe safely.

Medical science actually documents a physical reaction to sorrow. The body actually experiences a decrease in the production of white blood cells, which act as the body's defenders, fighting off colds and infections.[2] Ironically, isn't that exactly what our enemy would like to see happen with us? When the pressure and struggles of life *press* against us, wouldn't the enemy like us to quit on our purpose? Quit on our dreams?

Quit on our determination to finish life strong? Spiritually, sorrow weakens our defenses and attempts to take the hope out of our faith. Sorrow will try and steal your fight!

Here I was sitting in the airport trying to find the quickest way back to Josiah, feeling as though I couldn't breath, hearing the words "They're saying the worst" ring in my head and not knowing what the outcome was going to be. I didn't have a choir with me to help me begin to worship. There wasn't a pastor or a prayer line I could walk up to for support. All of the normal support systems were not available. All I had was the red carpet in terminal A of the airport, and I fell to my knees and began to cry out to God. I didn't care who could hear me. I didn't care who was watching. I didn't care what I looked like or what other people thought of me. I was crying out for the life of my son. I was experiencing a pressing, and I knew I needed to *press* back! Though it felt like forty-five years, there were about forty-five minutes where I was sitting in the airport, not knowing if my son would ever walk again, trying to find a chartered flight to the hospital and believing and praying for a miracle for my son.

I can only imagine how God felt as He watched Jesus suffer on the cross for you and me. No matter how many altar calls I have given, the words "His only begotten Son" had new meaning for me that day in the airport.

ALLOW THE PRESS TO REFINE YOUR PURPOSE

I love stories of fighters, people who overcome great odds and finish strong. That's what life is all about—fighting through the seasons of pressing and coming out stronger on the other side. My desire is that you take this book and read it to build your faith through your season of pressing and that you find the courage to push through the pain and reach the victory on the other side. I think, as people, sometimes the biggest lie we can buy into is the one that says, "It's over. This is it! My time is done. I'm too old. I don't have the resources. Nobody's looking for someone like me. I've lost someone I loved. How can I continue?" Just because you're experiencing a pressing doesn't mean your purpose has passed. Oftentimes your pressing is refining your purpose, and you must fight through the pressing to reach the prize. Philippians 3:14 says, "I press toward the mark for the prize of the high calling of God in Christ Jesus" (KJV). The process is oftentimes painful, but God can take what seems to be a mess and make it beautiful. Ecclesiastes 3:11 says, "He has made everything beautiful in its time. Also He has put eternity in their hearts, except that no one can find out the work that God does from beginning to end." We can't always see the full picture or how God is going to work it out.

Although "the press" can be painful at times, sometimes the sweetest and best things are produced only after being pressed. Take, for a small example, the process of harvesting Mediterranean olive oil, one of the best and most flavorful oils around. The Mediterranean olive tree must first mature for several years before even producing olives worthy of this oil. Careful attention is paid to proper pruning in order to produce quality oil and the most abundant olives per branch. It requires ten pounds of olives to produce only four cups of oil! Once the olives are ripe, the harvesters must vigorously shake the trees to drop the fruit and begin the pressing quickly, so as to not lose any flavor or damage the quality in any way. The olives are then crushed, matted, pressed, and heated to squeeze any and all oil from the olive, and only then is it ready to be consumed. You know oil is symbolic of the Holy Spirit. If you've allowed yourself to mature, the pressing could be squeezing a sweet, flavorful anointing from your life!

I played some basketball growing up and continue to love the sport. I enjoy watching my sons play as well as following the NBA. You know your team is really determined to win when the coach calls for a full-court press. That means every guy is assigned to a player on the other team, and the ultimate goal is to defensively stick to your guy like glue. Wherever the player goes, the defense is right there with their hands in their face. Normally defense is played from half-court and back, but during a press, the defense extends the length of the entire court. Interestingly a full-court press is implemented only when the opposing team is behind or the game is seriously close. The other team knows you have a chance of winning and the goal of the press is to stop you from winning. The goal is to wear out the opposing team. The goal is to get in the other team's head mentally. When life applies a full-court press, the goal is to wear you out! Don't get confused and think the game is over. It's just a press!

THE PRESS REQUIRES THE ANOINTING

I'm reminded of two stories in 2 Kings 4 with the prophet Elisha and two different women who experienced two different types of pressing. The first woman found herself newly widowed with no life insurance money and a pile of bills to pay, and her husband's creditor pursuing her sons to be his slaves to cover her debts. Listen to what the Bible says:

> One day the wife of a man from the guild of prophets
> called out to Elisha, "Your servant my husband is dead.
> You well know what a good man he was, devoted to
> GOD. And now the man to whom he was in debt is on
> his way to collect by taking my two children as slaves."
> —2 KINGS 4:1, THE MESSAGE

This lady was literally broke and, I'm sure, emotionally broken. She just lost her husband, which represented her present, and was about to lose her sons, which represented her future. Everything she knew to be her security was removed in a single day. She was pressed on all sides. I'm sure she thought life was over for her. As she approached Elisha, this is what he said to her:

> "I wonder how I can be of help. Tell me, what do you
> have in your house?" "Nothing," she said. "Well, I do
> have a little oil."
> —2 KINGS 4:2, THE MESSAGE

Here we are back to the oil! This lady has no real social status to speak of and is now in jeopardy of losing the only thing she has left, her sons. She is pressed on all sides only to find out when she was squeezed she has a little oil. She's got a little anointing. She was squeezed and life was pressing her in every direction, but in the midst of the squeeze she discovered all she needed was the Holy Spirit!

Now fast-forward in 2 Kings to the story immediately following the widow's story, and you come to 2 Kings 4:8 with a woman referred to as the Shunammite woman. Interestingly enough, the Shunammite is referred to as a rich and influential woman. She was obviously the opposite of the widow woman, and yet they both encountered a "pressing" in life that required the anointing.

The Bible says the Shunammite took notice that the prophet Elisha was a man of God. She and her husband designated a special "guest room" in their house for Elisha to stay as he would often pass through town to minister. Obviously proactive, this lady was quite the community organizer, I'm sure. She was the type of individual who had answers before problems even appeared. She was the lady who had dinner on the table every night, was involved in her community, volunteered at her church, always returned her Blockbuster movies on time, and never had a hair out of place! She probably had her life figured out, a solid IRA for retirement, and donated blood at the Red Cross at least two times a year. You get the picture. The Shunammite had her act together. Because of her kindness and generosity Elisha asks her one day what he can do in exchange for her hospitality. Listen to their conversation:

> Then he said to his servant Gehazi, "Tell the Shunammite woman I want to see her." He called her and she came to him. Through Gehazi Elisha said, "You've gone far beyond the call of duty in taking care of us; what can we do for you? Do you have a request we can bring to the king or to the commander of the army?" She replied, "Nothing. I'm secure and satisfied in my family." Elisha conferred with Gehazi: "There's got to be something we can do for her. But what?" Gehazi said, "Well, she has no son, and her husband is an old man."
>
> —2 Kings 4:13–14, The Message

Elisha prophesies that the woman would have a son within a year's time, and, sure enough, she gives birth to a son. Now you must imagine what this boy meant to the Shunammite. She was never supposed to have children and thought it was impossible because her husband was too old to have babies, and yet miraculously she receives a son, who became her entire world. Her son was the manifestation of her promise—a visible sign of God's favor and faithfulness in her life.

Several years later her son was working in the field with his father, and he gets a headache. The father sends his son back to his mother, and the Bible says the Shunammite's son died in her arms at *noon*. Her promise, her gift, her legacy died in her arms. I find it interesting that the Bible mentions the time as being noon. Noon is the middle of the day—the break between morning and evening, a shift from the sun rising to the sun setting. Noon is symbolic of the change of time. *The pressing always signifies a change in the time or season.*

The Bible says the Shunammite took her son, went and laid him on the bed of the prophet, and asked her husband to get the car ready, metaphorically speaking. Listen:

> She took him up and laid him on the bed of the man of God, shut him in alone, and left. She then called her husband, "Get me a servant and a donkey so I can go to the Holy Man; I'll be back as soon as I can."
> —2 Kings 4:21, The Message

Just like the widow woman referenced earlier, the Shunammite knew she needed the anointing during her time of pressing. She may not have had it in her house, but she knew where to find it, and she knew she couldn't waste time getting to it. You may have strayed from God. Maybe you're not as close as you once were. Maybe you grew up in the church but you really haven't pursued a relationship with Jesus. Maybe the business of life has gotten in the way and a pressing in your life has you looking for the anointing. Just like the Shunamite, you can always find the anointing. *The pressing requires the anointing!*

Once the Shunammite reached Elisha, I think her response is similar to our natural inclination as human beings. Listen to what the woman says as she reaches the prophet:

> Then she spoke up: "Did I ask you for a son, master? Didn't I tell you, 'Don't tease me with false hopes'?"
> —2 KINGS 4:28, THE MESSAGE

I believe what she was saying was, "God, how could You let my dreams die? How could this make sense? A promise You made to me has ended in disaster." Everything in front of the Shunammite indicated it was over. Finality. No hope. Gone. But here is what we have to understand about the pressing. *The pressing, though we can't determine the outcome, requires that we press back!*

Look at how the Shunammite presses back when Elisha wants to send his servant Gehazi to pray for her son:

> He ordered Gehazi, "Don't lose a minute—grab my staff and run as fast as you can. If you meet anyone, don't even take time to greet him, and if anyone greets you, don't even answer. Lay my staff across the boy's face." The boy's mother said, "As sure as GOD lives

and you live, you're not leaving me behind." And so
Gehazi let her take the lead, and followed behind.
—2 KINGS 4:29–30, THE MESSAGE

The Shunammite was basically saying, "Listen, I'm not
letting go of my promise. I'm not letting go of my legacy and
my dream. God spoke this to me, and I'm clinging onto it
with every bit of fiber in my body."

There are some people who get confused and quit on their
purpose when life presses against them. You must understand that the pressing will purify the product! Those who
quit in the midst of the process and misunderstand the season
in which they stand have a tendency to allow bitterness to
take root in their lives and hearts. Hold fast in the season
of pressing and understand that God is faithful, despite what
things look like in the natural!

POSTURE YOURSELF TOWARD THE PRESS

Have you ever started a new workout routine? If you haven't
worked out in a while, it is a bit intimidating to walk into a
facility such as Gold's Gym or Family Fitness, especially if
you are working out in the weight-lifting area. The bulging
pectorals and oversized biceps could immediately discourage
you, if you're just beginning to work out and your muscles are
less than developed. But I've learned it is much easier if you
posture yourself toward the press.

As I mentioned earlier in the canoeing story with my son
and me, in order to get out into the ocean past the breaking
waves, we had to point our canoe straight into the oncoming
waves. Any angle would have flipped our boat. So it is with

life. It might be difficult and a bit intimidating, like starting a new workout, but you have to face the pressing head-on. You have to walk into the press with confidence knowing your goal is the other side.

I've been told life can be equated to a series of steps ranging from one to ten. Consider the fundamentals of life as steps you ascend as you learn and grow with each new step taking you higher. Oftentimes step ten is the pinnacle of your achievements. But as you go through life, climbing the ladder looking to achieve number ten, something inevitable happens. Once you conquer the number ten, you start at one again. It might be twenty-one or thirty-one or eighty-one, but it's the same principles of your original number one.

How frustrating, you might say. It's still the same fundamentals of your very first one. Naturally you want growth and development and new levels. The principles for each step remain the same and the fundamentals remain the same, but on each new level you have a little more depth and a little more influence. As you grow, learn, and develop, you might reach a new level, but you are always cycling one through ten with the same fundamentals.

When you recognize and understand the cycle and seasons of your life, the press becomes nothing more than a workout and a time of training and conditioning. Press on with confidence. You have a race to finish!

Here my wife, Jennette, gives her account of when she walked into the hospital the day of the accident:

> I came rushing into the hospital to find Josiah. The children's hospital was about a forty-minute drive

from my house, but I made it that day in about thirty minutes by the grace of God. A friend was driving me, and I remember just sitting in the passenger seat, crying and praying, "God, please don't let my baby die. God, please let my baby walk and lead a normal life." I had received a few phone calls from some dear pastor friends who prayed with me over the phone and spoke life over Josiah and his body. The feeling was surreal to run into the hospital and hear Josiah was checked in under the name "Trauma Juneau." Whenever a severe patient is admitted or transported via life flight, the hospital assigns a trauma name to the patient for quick and easy admission. I was looking for Josiah, my baby, but the hospital staff knew him as "Trauma Juneau."

I was quickly escorted into the emergency room and saw Josiah lying on the cold hospital table. His shirt had been cut from him, and several medical staff members were all around running tests and evaluating his condition. He was stabilized on a medical board and was supported with a neck brace. The first thing I wanted to do was touch him and look into his eyes and let him see I was there with him. It was heart wrenching to put him into the helicopter and hear him say, "Mommy, please don't leave me," but there were restrictions on the helicopter and there wasn't enough room for another adult, so I had to release him to the flight crew. Time was of the essence. Josiah's eyes were still. He wasn't crying, but looking into them you could tell he understood the severity of the situation. Despite Josiah's concern, there seemed to be a peace in his eyes.

The doctors hadn't given us any indication as to Josiah's evaluation yet. He was responding well and moving his extremities, but nothing was determined and no results had been released to us concerning his long-term condition. Family, friends, and pastors we knew from all across the country were praying for Josiah and believing for total restoration. We believed he was going to be OK, but we just wanted to hear something from the doctors. We just wanted to hear Josiah would lead a normal life.

Jennette and I were standing on the only thing we had, which was our faith, but waiting to hear a report from the doctor was one of the hardest things we've had to do.

2

THE WAITING ROOM OF LIFE

"When the waiting time is over, battles fought and vict'ries won, we shall hear the Savior's welcome, 'Good and faithful one, well done.'"[1]

EVERY TIME THERE seems to be a pressing in your life, you can be sure "the waiting room" is going to follow. Ironically, while I was waiting at the airport to get back to my son in the hospital, more than fifty wheelchairs surrounded me in the terminal where I was sitting. It just so happened that I was sitting in the storage area for the handicap resources at the airport. Talk about messing with my emotions! I literally had to fight the thoughts that I may have to push Josiah around in a wheelchair for the rest of his life or help my son walk with a breathing machine or a breathing tube coming from his neck. So many thoughts and pictures were messing with my head in those minutes. I did the only thing I could at the time, and I fell on my face before God in that very terminal in utter surrender and prayer—waiting on God to speak.

How You Wait Will Determine Your Fate

"Statisticians have estimated that in a lifetime of 70 years, the average person spends at least three years waiting."[2] Waiting has to be one of the most excruciating events in life, yet it is what you *do* while waiting that can push the victory forward. As a technology-driven universe, we're not trained to wait. In fact, we merely "push a button" and expect to have the answer immediately in front of us. We even grow impatient standing in line, so we order what we need online. With Google and Wikipedia so readily available, information is flooding us constantly. But waiting must be a learned activity. Waiting must be intentional. Waiting must be developed. In the midst of every crisis, you have to make a choice as to whether you're going to follow your own instincts or seek God's guidance to do it His way.

Waiting is trust. Waiting is belief. Waiting is being anxious at nothing. In fact, waiting is patience, and patience is more than endurance. There are going to be some valleys in life for all of us. I love what it says in John 16:33, "In this world you will have trouble. But take heart! I have overcome the world" (NIV). The basic question is not how dark your valleys will be, but rather how will you react and wait while you are in the valley?

Waiting is an interesting concept that is deliberate and intentional. The vibrant lifestyles of today's society adhere to the fact that it is easy to be distracted from the simplicity of dependence on God. Without purposefully waiting upon the Lord, you will be pulled in many different, distracting directions. However, there truly is something powerful that happens when you choose to get quiet before the Lord and wait upon Him. When you pull yourself away from the hustle and bustle of life, God can and will speak and change your destiny and course of direction—"Be still and know" that God is in control. How you wait can determine your fate!

When I was a much younger man, a few years out of high school, I worked for a produce company and drove a produce truck to pay bills while I was attending college. I hadn't been saved very long, and I recently had gotten involved at my church where I was helping with the music and youth departments. I knew God hadn't called me to drive lettuce around for the rest of my life, but it was a job that was making ends meet until the next door opened.

I'll never forget one night at church. At first it just seemed to be a normal service. I played guitar for the worship set and was getting ready to sit down when the pastor looked at me and said, "Ricardo, God is going to take you to the nations of the world. There is an anointing on you for the body of Christ. Get ready. You'll go around the globe from China to Africa to Europe." Wow, I left church that night barely able to sleep! I was sure Billy Graham's office would be calling me in the morning for their next crusade to Africa. But the next morning at 4:00 a.m. my alarm went off reminding me that the lettuce and carrots in the back of my truck needed to be delivered to the local restaurants or I would be fired.

A day or two went by, and still there were no phone calls

for the "anointing" on the inside of me. One week went by. Another week went by and still no phone calls. Week after week I was standing on God's Word. I believed there was more inside of me than lettuce, but frustration was setting in. I'll never forget one day driving in Phoenix finishing my delivery rounds, and I was so overcome with despair. "God, have You forgotten me? God, is this really my destiny? God, where are You?" I know the people driving next to me had to have thought I had lost my mind, but I didn't care. I began literally talking to God and began to thank Him for where He placed me. I changed from despair to repair. "God, I thank You for this job. God, even if I'm here five more years, I'll do it with joy and excellence. God, if I have to, I'll get some cucumbers saved."

You get the picture. I began to change my waiting period into worship, and I believe my worship got God's attention. I promise you it wasn't a few days later and I received a phone call from my pastor to come on full-time staff at the church. I wasn't traveling the globe yet, but it was a step toward God's direction for my life. How you *wait* can determine your *fate*.

SILENCE THE "EMOTION COMMOTION"

Have you ever noticed that emotions can speak to you in the "waiting room" of life's battles? That's certainly what my emotions were doing when I was waiting to hear what the doctors' report was on Josiah. Your emotions can tell you what you see in the natural and what you may be feeling, but your emotions don't always line up with God's Word. Your emotions can cloud your view of reality. I call it "emotion commotion." You have to battle through your moods into absolute devotion to God and remove yourself from the moment or your current situation and into abandoned communion with Him. It is important to remember that "if you do not stand firm in your faith, you will not stand at all" (Isa. 7:9, NIV). Not giving into the thoughts of despair and destruction that surely will try and attack your mind is a difficult yet conscientious choice. You must teach your emotions to fight right and to fight with faith.

Every person must be prepared for life's difficult seasons. It is in those seasons that your emotions will reveal their foundation. Are they rooted in God's Word, or are they rooted in fear and worry? Your emotions are the truest test of character and even motive. Under the strain of the disaster, stress, or pressure, some people turn to God; some people turn to human wisdom; and yet some people will give up and become bitter against God. Your emotions can clog the flow of God's anointing if you don't harness and direct your emotions to line up with God's Word.

David, one of my favorite people in the Bible, experienced many catastrophes and many trials and was a great example of taming the "emotion commotion." David was a young man who was greatly loved by God and is mentioned more than one thousand times in the Bible. David's skill, which he learned, developed, and demonstrated during times of calamity and struggle, allowed and enabled him to maintain a right spirit, one of joyfulness, no matter the circumstance.

David, "a man after God's own heart," was himself a simple shepherd, yet he became the "Shepherd King" of Israel. As a fellow musician I can relate to the meditations, songs, and even cries of David. But David was familiar with difficult situations, dangers, and even misunderstandings. As a young shepherd boy David fought wild animals that attempted to prey on his father's flock. Later, as a young man, he challenged the giant Goliath in hand-to-hand combat. Even after all of this David's oldest brother, Eliab, misunderstood his intentions and accused him of having a prideful heart. After having been through all this, David's great victories in battle were interpreted as a threat by King Saul and his motivations were misjudged. (See 1 Samuel 18.) However, despite the rejection of those around him, David maintained a cheerful spirit, and he "encouraged himself in the LORD" (1 Sam. 30:6, KJV). He got quiet and sought the hand of God. Sure, David's successes in battle were unrivaled, his ability with weapons was intriguing, and his people skills were amazing, but it was his ability to turn to God whenever he experienced sorrow or despair that makes him such an example of success.

Of the many great David stories in the Bible, there is a story that I love in 1 Samuel 30:1–20 that challenged me in my time of waiting. David and his six hundred men were just returning home to Ziklag—a city that David lived in first because he had to flee King Saul, and second because he was able to launch raids against invaders of his country. Upon returning home, he and his men found that their homes had been destroyed and all their women and children had been taken captive by the Amalekites. David's situation was very foreboding, but David knew that the only thing he could do was to wait on God's direction. "David and his men wept aloud until they had no strength left to weep" (1 Sam. 30:4, NIV).

How quickly the situation changed and turned out of control. Just a short time before people were chanting, "Saul has slain his thousands, and David his tens of thousands" (1 Sam. 18:7, NIV). This man had known the praise and acceptance of a nation; then shortly thereafter David was rejected by King Saul, whom he had faithfully served. All he had left was his family and his six hundred faithful companions. Now he had lost his family, and his men wanted to kill him because they doubted his leadership. Listen to what the Bible says: "David was greatly distressed because his men were talking of stoning him; each one was bitter in spirit because of his sons and daughters" (1 Sam. 30:6, NIV).

Because David trained his emotions to fight right, he encouraged himself in the Lord. David's men watched and grew silent. Their mood changed, and soon there was a different spirit in David's army. Your emotions can change the atmosphere! While the Amalekites were in excessive celebration over the conquest of Ziklag, God led David and his men in a fierce battle as they overtook their attackers. Not only did they win, but they were also able to rescue all of their captives and recover all of their possessions. The Lord God provided a solution. A solution that required a "stillness." A solution that required strength and confidence in their faith. A solution that required waiting on God. And a solution that ultimately led to victory.

In a situation like the story mentioned above with David, Elijah would have sat down under a juniper tree and waited to die (1 Kings 19:4), Job's wife would have cursed God and died (Job 2:9), Jonah would have claimed it to be better to die than to live (Jon. 4:8), and King Saul would have consulted the pagan witch of Endor to console him (1 Sam. 28). "But David encouraged himself in the LORD his God" (1 Sam.

30:6, KJV). David always directed his emotions to trust in God. Interestingly enough, it was shortly after this battle at Ziklag that King Saul was killed in battle and David became the anointed king of Israel. Listen to what David writes after walking through all of this:

> God set things right for me and shut up the people who talked back. He rescued me from enemy anger, he pulled me from the grip of upstarts, He saved me from the bullies. That's why I'm thanking you, God, all over the world. That's why I'm singing songs.
> —Psalm 18: 47–49, The Message

David walked through trials and was betrayed on countless occasions. He experienced many of the same issues you and I face, even to a greater degree, in many cases. But David knew how to wait on God and allowed God to work in his situation for the glory of God. Read what David penned in Psalm 40:1–3:

> I waited patiently for the Lord; and He inclined to me, and He heard my cry. He also brought me up out of a horrible pit, out of the miry clay, and set my feet upon a rock and established my steps. He has put a new song in my mouth.

David's feet were set upon a rock and his steps were established. When you wait patiently on the Lord, all the ups and downs of emotions are settled and set firmly on the rock of God. Though, at times, David's emotions were all over the place and his road wasn't always easy, David learned to trust in his Savior. Silence your "emotion commotion" and wait on the presence of God to work all things for His glory!

There is an old Jewish proverb that says, "Patience is half of wisdom." If you have enough wisdom to wait for God, He will provide you with the other half of the wisdom that you need. God wants you to slow down enough so you can hear the sound of His still, small voice. Spending time with God in your daily, sometimes mundane, routine will keep you fed and built up so that you have the strength to "run and not grow weary" and keep your emotions from running all over the place.

THE SOUND OF WAITING

When I was growing up in Arizona, it was my mother's Saturday routine to visit the flea market or swap meet in our community and shop at the local farmers' and merchants' booths. One morning she was determined to find a wind chime to hang on our back porch. As we strolled the aisles looking for the right vendor, my mom spotted her wind chime. We walked into the vendor's tent that housed nearly one hundred different chimes. My mother picked up her desired prize and began to admire its beauty. I could tell she was picturing the chime on our back porch.

Almost immediately after my mother picked up the piece, the owner turned and said he would be unable to sell us that particular chime. Having visited the same flea market every Saturday for several years, I knew those merchants were there to make money. I was confused, and by the obvious look on my mother's face, she was confused too. Perplexed by the situation, she immediately asked, "Why not?" The gentleman began to explain, "I hand make all of the wind chimes in this tent, and I can tell by the sound the chime is making if there are any cracks in the surface of the chime. If there are, the chime will gradually crack, which would eventually cause it to crumble." Still not sure if my mother was following the man's reasoning, I continued to listen to his explanation. "As the maker of the chime, I know the sound the chime is supposed to make. Though a crack might not be visible to the naked eye, its sound will give away its flaw and any adversity will cause the chime to fall apart! The chime you have chosen is defective, and I can tell by the sound."

Just like the maker of the wind chimes, I believe your Maker is listening to the sound you make during the waiting periods of life. Are you whining while you wait? Are you complaining while you wait? Are you grumbling while you wait? Is fear controlling you while you wait?

Isn't that what the wilderness experience was all about for the Israelites? The Israelites were in the wilderness for forty years, but it was really only an eleven-day journey to the Promise Land (Deut. 1:2). Immediately following the Israelites' victorious exodus from Egypt through the Red Sea, the same Israelites began to grumble and complain because they were unsure where their provision and sustenance would come from next, even though they had just watched God part a body of water where approximately two to three million Israelites crossed on dry ground. They just watched God split the Red Sea, which was estimated to be a little over 650 feet deep where they crossed. Yes, the Red Sea was held apart by the hand of God while several million Israelites crossed on dry ground. Do you understand that if God parted the

Red Sea at this depth, it would be the equivalent of half of the Empire State Building! That's about fifty-one stories high! Can you imagine seeing a wall of water half the height of the Empire State Building being held back for a few hours? The width of the area where the Israelites crossed is estimated to be about 262 feet; that's about three-fourths the length of a standard American football field. The waters had to have been sustained for several hours to see that many people cross in an area just smaller than a football field.

Are you kidding me! This was no small miracle. Some scholars believe that the Israelites crossed the Red Sea during the rainy season and that the banks of the Red Sea were over-flowing, indicating it was even deeper than normal. I don't want to beat a dead horse, but I want you to see this picture. The Israelites just walked through on dry ground with "water walls" fifty-one stories high on either side and not even their clothes got wet, yet the Israelites were immediately complaining about what they were going to eat for breakfast the next morning!

Let's put that in perspective with kids, either your own or someone else's children you've been around. You know how you feel when you give and give and give and all you hear is complaining. It's just like with God. God is listening to the sound of your waiting. Your sound will reveal your heart, and your sound will reveal whom you trust. Refine your sound and keep your song in tune with God!

WAIT AND RENEW

Oftentimes it is easy to be tempted to fill your time of waiting with meaningless activities. Waiting is not always easy.

Whether it's golf or shopping or talking with your friends, sometimes those activities are nothing more than time fillers and distractions. Please hear my heart. I am all for relaxing and enjoying life, but if you are in a season of "it's not over," you must diligently wait on God. It is the very command of "wait" that truly pushes you to victory. The Bible says, "Those who wait on the LORD shall renew their strength; they shall mount up with wings like eagles, they shall run and not be weary" (Isa. 40:31).

Scripture often contains parallels with the majestic appearances and awesome skills of the eagle to symbolize important truths for God's people. What is more amazing is the God-given design of the eagle! The eagle is designed to achieve its full potential through the disciplines that are required of it in simplicity, stillness, and even adversity. Violent storms push the eagle to reach its highest heights; scarcity of food forces the eagle to develop its sharp eyesight, amazing speed, and accurate diving; and the eagle's lonely environment allows the bird to care for its mate and to skillfully train its young.

Contrary to society's teaching of creating your own opportunities, waiting is a learned, active behavior—not passive! In order to renew your strength, you must wait on God through actions such as prayer, fasting, worship, and meditation on His Word. This is what renews your strength—not golfing, not shopping. The deliberate act of waiting requires devotion, intentionality, and discipline. *Actively* waiting on the Lord will renew your strength to soar like an eagle and run the race God has set before you.

I've often heard it paralleled that you must wait on God just like a waiter would wait on you in a nice restaurant or a servant would wait on the king. "Father, do You need anything else today? God, who do You want me to serve today? Lord, can I do anything for You? God, do You want me to go in this direction or that direction? I'm going to wait until You call me. I'm going to wait until You tell me to go."

There are stories rooted in the heritage of America's pioneer past that contain many characters who sought and depended solely on God's provision and deliverance through adversity. One great example that I love is the New Hampshire folktale known as the "Sarah Whitcher Story." This story has been passed on from generation to generation in order to attest to the miracles of God and the power of faith—the courage and resourcefulness of a little lost girl, the steadfast faith of her father, and a stranger's obedience to God by way of a dream.

This story was set around the 1870s in an area know as the Warren Settlement. The Warren Settlement was located in the region known today as New Hampshire. At that time the area was very primitive and underdeveloped, so each family honored the Sabbath in their homes and in their own unique way because no buildings had been erected yet to serve as a formal church setting. The Whitcher family was no different. They spent their Sabbath Sundays studying God's Word and enjoying nature together as a family. Under the direction of their father, the Whitcher family practiced "in everything give thanks" and "trust only in the Lord." Little did they know that this way of believing, thinking, and living would be put to the test.

Curious and ambitious, young Sarah followed a flitting bird away from her cabin and become distracted and pulled away when she found a strawberry patch and flowers. All this continued to draw Sarah into a thick, unsettled forest far away from her home. As the night began to fall, Sarah finally realized she was lost, but she believed that her trusty dog, Ollie, was there with her. Though Ollie smelt strange to Sarah and was even rough with her, which was not Ollie's normal tendencies, the warmth of his body made Sarah feel safe and secure in a dark and lonely forest. Meanwhile, settlers begin gathering at her family's farm to begin searching for Sarah. Mr. Whitcher made sure Ollie remained at the cabin to protect the family while he went off into the woods. So who or what was caring for Sarah?

After four long days of trudging through the woods, the search group began to lose hope and was certain that there was no way that a five-year-old child could survive the cold without food and water. Many people committed to search during the day in hopes of merely finding Sarah's remains and offer closure to her family. Only Sarah's father trusted that they would find her alive and continued to seek God. Sarah's father refused to allow the worry to control him in the midst of the wait, and he renewed his strength by staying in God's Word.

Finally, on the fifth day, a strange man arrived in the Warren settlement. His name was Mr. Heath. He had walked thirty miles from Plymouth because of a very specific, detailed dream. In his dream a bear was nightly caring for a little red-headed girl by leading her to a berry patch and then to a cave. He could explain the exact location but did not know how to get there. Doubtful of his information, a few searchers guided him as he explained the scene and topography of his dream. As they neared the area that he envisioned in the dream, Mr.

Heath was able to walk right to where little Sarah was lying with the bear nearby. Feeble and weak, yes, but definitely alive! And as soon as Mr. Heath and the others took her home, her father said, "Amen. I didn't know what the Lord would do or how He would do it, but I knew He would do something." Then the family sang "Praise God From Whom All Blessings Flow." Amazing, isn't it?

While preaching in Indonesia recently, a very familiar story from the Bible caught my eye with new and profound insight. Acts 16 tells the story of Paul and Silas being thrown into a Roman prison. As Roman citizens, this represented a grave injustice. They were beaten based on false charges, and with wounds untreated, Paul and Silas were thrown into the dark, inner prison and bound in stocks as though they were dangerous criminals. But instead of filling the midnight hour with groans and justifiable complaints, Paul and Silas *prayed* and sang praises to God (Acts 16:25). Read what the Bible says in Acts 16:26–30 as the story continues to unfold:

> Suddenly there was a great earthquake, so that the foundations of the prison were shaken; and immediately all the doors were opened and everyone's chains were loosed. And the keeper of the prison, awaking from sleep and seeing the prison doors open, supposing the prisoners had fled, drew his sword and was about to kill himself. But Paul called with a loud voice, saying, "Do yourself no harm, for we are all here." Then he called for a light, ran in, and fell down trembling before Paul and Silas. And he brought them out and said, "Sirs, what must I do to be saved?"

I have always read and understood Paul and Silas began to worship, and it was their worship that caused the earthquake, which, in turn, caused the prison doors to break open. However, this time when I read the text, I realized it was what Paul and Silas *did* with their waiting period that produced their victory. Paul and Silas were not distracted by the worldly cares in the prison. They were removed, almost set apart, and they prayed *then* sang praises to God. They had the ability to rejoice when everyone else was discouraged; they produced joy in the lives of others because they were able to rejoice in the cruelest possible circumstances. They renewed their strength through prayer, and that strength was transmitted to those around them. I too want to pass the test as one of God's own who innately and immediately cries out to Him in prayer and worship during times of struggle.

There is something that happens when you get quiet with God and pray. Several times throughout the Bible God would speak to men while they were asleep, unable to rationalize the voice of God. I believe their slumber represented a removal from their daily routine. They couldn't outthink what God was saying or somehow talk themselves out of the direction God was leading them.

In Genesis 15 God spoke to Abraham in a dream while he was asleep and promised his seed would be as the sands of the seashore. While Adam was asleep, God pulled his future from his side and gave him Eve (Gen. 2:21–22). In Genesis 28 while Jacob was asleep, God gave him a vision of the open heavens and promised provision. God will speak to you in the waiting periods of your life, but you must remove yourself from the distractions and worldly chaos to get quiet with Him. That is where your strength will come from.

WATER THE WAIT

I love the story of the Chinese bamboo tree, which demonstrates the importance of "watering during the wait." The bamboo tree must be planted in the right soil, watered, and tended to daily. For one whole year you must water and wait on your tree, but you must know, no growth will happen. Not one single bud or twig will sprout. So yet another year will pass with you protecting and watering the tree, but again not a single sign of growth. One would assume that nothing is happening. Visibly no growth appears. For three more years the pattern continues: you water, you wait, and nothing.

By the time the fifth year rolls around, you're not sure you even think you should pay this little tree any more attention. With one last glimpse of hope, you decide to give this little tree one more year. You water and wait yet one more time. Then one morning in the fifth year, you go to water the tree again, and much to your surprise, you see a green stem shooting from the soil! Excitement builds, so you ambitiously continue to nurture your little tree. The bamboo tree does something amazing. Within six weeks the bamboo tree that did nothing for five years shoots to over eighty feet tall![3] Wow! That is exactly what waiting through life's circumstances is often like. It appears that nothing is happening. You can't see any visible signs of growth, yet if at any point in the five-year period you stopped watering the tree, the tree would have died. You must continue to water your life with the Word of God and believe

He is at work in your life and situation even when it appears nothing is happening! Water during the waiting!

The Bible says in Proverbs 18:21, "Death and life are in the power of the tongue, and those who love it will eat its fruit." I love The Message translation, which says, "Words kill, words give life; they're either poison or fruit—you choose." Your words will *water* your life while you wait or your words will *starve* your life while you wait. You decide.

THE ALTITUDE ADJUSTMENT

In the Christian life there is frequent talk of wanting to "move to higher ground with God." As people it is only natural to long to live above the lowlands, to live beyond the common and enter a more intimate walk with God. People speak and sing of the mountaintops, and sometimes it can be easy to envy those who have ascended the heights of a sublime sort of life. Somehow as natural human beings it is easy to get this erroneous idea about how this ascension to the mountaintop takes place. It is as though people sometimes think that they can be airlifted onto higher ground. But being airlifted would merely cheat you from the very necessary process called the "altitude adjustment."

Did you know that there is an actual adjustment your physical body must make when ascending into higher altitudes? At higher altitudes there is less oxygen and less barometric pressure, which makes it more difficult for your body to breathe and transport oxygen. There is an actual sickness known as "altitude sickness" that can occur when you are not accustomed to living at higher altitudes. I find it ironic that a few of the symptoms that can occur with altitude sickness are fatigue, shortness of breath, and loss of energy.

Just as it is physically, so it is spiritually. If you have not trained your spiritual body to live at higher heights, you can get altitude sickness with the same symptoms—tired, spiritually burnt out, loss of breath, no love to share with others, and no energy to finish the fight. You must wait on God to adjust your altitude! You can only climb to the mountaintop through prayer and spending time with Him.

Yes, every high mountain has its valleys, and it is this very gradual, winding path that starts in the valley that gets you to the top safely. In the midst of the climb you might say what Jennette and I have often said, "Oh, God, this road is hard. This is the toughest thing we've ever been through." It is at this very confession during the dark times that I have discovered that God is there with me in my distress, teaching me necessary adjustments for the next incline. God promises in Psalm 34:19 that "a righteous man may have many troubles, but the Lord delivers him from them all." *All* of them! At that point in the airport when I gave my panic and my fear to God, a sense of calm and quiet confidence consumed me and I was in His care—just as Josiah was in His care. Somehow, in a serene and quiet way, I became assured of His control all over again.

We had learned from the EMTs who assisted in transporting Josiah via helicopter that there was less than a 1 percent survival rate for people with Josiah's type of spinal injury. Josiah had broken his C3, C4, C5, and C6 cervical spinal nerves in his neck when he dove into the bottom of the pool. These cervical nerves housed inside the C3-C5 vertebrae innervate the thoracic diaphragm. There was a mnemonic utilized by medical students, paramedics, and the fire department to remember the danger involved when the C4 nerve gets damaged. The saying goes, "Break C4, breathe no more." This mnemonic was used as a reminder for medical staff to remember how vital and important the C4 and above vertebras are. Simply put, the C4 controlled Josiah's breathing. Any bone broken above the C4 clavicle meant incredibly slim odds of leading a normal life without the continuous assistance of ventilators and breathing machines, much less surviving.

It was after about forty-five minutes of waiting at the airport that my phone rang. I was waiting to hear about a flight to get to the hospital in Atlanta, and if there would be a plane and a pilot available on such a short emergency notice, but it was Jennette on the other end of the phone. She had some news for me. She was still at the hospital and Josiah was in the emergency room still being evaluated by several specialists, neurosurgeons, and doctors. They had sedated Josiah in order to minimize any movements and decrease the possibility of fractured bone pieces moving around any further. The doctors wanted to make sure the reports they brought back to Jennette were as accurate as possible.

Jennette called to tell me of a completely unexpected phone call that again brought me to my knees in the airport. Ironically we had a family member in California who happened to be at the house of a prestigious and well-recognized neurosurgeon. After hearing the news of Josiah's accident, he immediately got on the phone and began requesting Josiah's test results and X-rays for evaluation and recommendations. While we were anxiously awaiting *any* news at all from the doctors at our hospital about Josiah's long-term conditions, God had arranged for the best team of doctors all across the country to assist Josiah. Jennette's phone rang, and the first words she heard from the neurosurgeon were, "Jennette, I want you to know, your son is going to walk again!" Tears burst from Jennette's eyes as she received the miraculous report we had been waiting to hear! Praise God! If you could see me even now, you'd know I'm still shouting and still rejoicing at the grace of God. Josiah was going to be a walking, talking, breathing miracle! This season of waiting was over, but the journey was not yet finished. We had to first endure the surgery, physical therapy, and several weeks in the hospital.

3

THE STRENGTH OF STRUGGLE

"Thru many dangers, toils and snares I have already come. 'Tis grace hath bro't me safe thus far, and grace will lead me home."[1]

WILL NEVER FORGET about twelve years ago when I was first starting out in the Christian worship world and nobody really knew who I was. I had just recorded my first record, but nobody cared what songs I had written. Nobody was calling to schedule me for their church conference or to help produce their record.

Jennette and I were newly married with one baby at the time, and we had an opportunity to be a "fly on the wall" during a radio program with gospel music legends Israel Houghton, Donnie McClurkin, and BeBe Winans. I was sitting in the interview listening to the exchange and the conversation as

Donnie McClurkin and BeBe Winans were interviewing Israel Houghton who, at the time, was an up-and-comer. I'll never forget something that Donnie said during the interview. The purpose of the interview was to find out how Israel was handling all the accolades and success he was receiving by his peers and the music world at large. Donnie said, "I am so grateful for the mountaintop experiences of where I am, but you know what, BeBe, I miss the fight!" And then he looked at Israel and said, "Enjoy the fight because you learn something in the fight that you wouldn't otherwise ever learn."

What he was saying was that when you're fighting for your life, fighting for your ministry, or fighting for your marriage, your finances, your kids, you are building muscles that you would otherwise never build. The mountaintop is beautiful, but you lose sight of the beauty along the way. Sometimes before there is a resurrection, there needs to be a crucifixion.

USE THE STRUGGLE FOR STRENGTH

Facing an "it's not over" moment will certainly throw you headlong into the workout room of struggle. *Struggle* is not a word that you put on your annual Christmas card, nor is it a word that brings to mind images of joy and laughter. But just as an athlete trains his physical body, so can struggle strengthen and train your spiritual body. Most everyone wants the glory of hard work, but very few are willing to commit to the process.

Jennette was a division-one collegiate athlete for volleyball and still has vivid memories of early predawn runs through the hills behind her campus, swimming laps and treading water until her fingers and toes looked like prunes, hours spent in the workout room, suicide drills, sprints, jumping rope, and lap after lap running the stairs of the baseball stadium. And this was just preseason conditioning! Muscle strains, aches and pains, blisters and bruises, ice packs and heat wraps all came with the territory of those first several weeks of training. But she also remembers how this strenuous effort—however unpleasant it was at the time—shaped and honed her muscles and lungs and prepared her both physically and mentally for the long and difficult matches she and her team would be engaged in against opposing teams throughout the season. On more than one occasion in those lengthy matches that found each team fighting tooth and nail for every point, the team that had made the extra effort weeks before in the preseason was the team that came out victorious.

There is a graduation that occurs at the end of struggle that can catapult you into your next season, if you allow it and surrender to it. The journey of struggle involves release. You must fling yourself into the arms of Jesus and trust He is at work in your situation.

When you release yourself to the process of struggle, you learn to fight. You develop muscle endurance and strength and gain a confidence in your mission and purpose. The process of release and letting go of your "it's not over" circumstance involves three steps: 1) being broken before God, 2) being rebuilt with His new strength, and 3) being resurrected in the next season of life. The Bible is a continued story about men and women being broken and surrendered to God, being rebuilt, and ultimately being resurrected into the next season of life. Time and time again we see illustrated in these vividly honest biographies how the process of being broken before God and being masterfully rebuilt in the power of His strength will resurrect us from our own unique and very personal "it's not over" circumstance as victors and overcomers.

Everyone wants the victory, but few are willing to go through the process of being broken. Look with me for a moment at some examples in the Bible of men and women who submitted their "it's not over" moment to God and allowed Him to rebuild their situation.

Though at no fault of his own, Job faced one of the most well-known and recounted trials in the history of mankind. He was broken and humbled before God and then—after a time—saw his health, family, wealth, possessions, and influence restored even greater than it was before.

Ruth lost her husband and was left a widow with no possibility of another husband. Yet when urged by her mother-in-law to return to the land of her own people, Ruth was determined to remain where God had placed her and soon thereafter married Boaz, who served as her kinsman redeemer.

The prophet Daniel was sentenced to death while in the service of a pagan king but had absolute confidence in God to deliver him. Daniel was not only delivered from the threatening jaws of the lions quite literally, if you recall, but he was also given authority to rule over that very same kingdom.

David was in exile, driven to find refuge in a cave on account of the rage of jealous King Saul, who had commanded an entire army to hunt him down. Yet David refused to kill Saul when he unexpectedly found himself in a position to do so in that same dark, damp cave, and he allowed God to promote him at the right time.

Paul, Gomer, Mary Magdalene, Esther, Matthew, Mark,

Luke, and John...from the Old Testament straight through the Gospels and the Epistles, the list goes on and on. As each person released their brokenness to God, they found strength in the process of struggle and came out stronger on the other side.

Now, please hear me; I am not advocating that God intentionally sends bad things (death, destruction, illness, calamity, heartache, tragedy, or loss) your way in order to teach you a lesson. In fact, I believe quite the opposite. The passage of Scripture in Matthew 7:7–11 is such a great image of our loving Father:

> Don't bargain with God. Be direct. Ask for what you need. This isn't a cat-and-mouse, hide-and-seek game we're in. If your child asks for bread, do you trick him with sawdust? If he asks for fish, do you scare him with a live snake on his plate? As bad as you are, you wouldn't think of such a thing. You're at least decent to your own children. So don't you think the God who conceived you in love will be even better?
>
> —The Message

As children of God we live in a fallen, not-yet-redeemed world. The bottom line is that stuff happens, and as long as we live and breathe in this world, we will encounter our fair share of stuff.

The Weight of the Workout

I can picture it almost this way. Not too long ago I took my family to an outdoor recreation area that had rock-climbing walls, zip lines, and a ropes course—an obstacle course designed to be traversed on cables suspended between trees or utility poles several feet above ground. After completing the ropes course and taking a ride on the zip line, we moved on to the rock climbing walls. When it was my youngest son Micah's turn to climb, he chose a rock wall that was visibly very difficult and probably not quite age appropriate for him. But Micah was insistent. That particular wall captivated his attention so much so that it seemed as if he were impervious to the degree of difficulty involved in successfully accomplishing this feat. I knew Micah would have to exercise muscles he had never used to climb this particular wall and, to me, would require instincts that typically take years of climbing experience to acquire. In fact, the rock wall was so steep at points that the climbers nearly inverted themselves as they ascended. I wasn't quite sure I myself could maneuver my way up that wall, much less my youngest son.

Yet as Micah's father I knew by allowing him to climb the rock wall he would not only build muscles, but more importantly, he would also build confidence. As the staff member was fitting Micah's safety harness and securing his belay, I could see my son's face begin to constrict as the color slowly ebbed from his cheeks. His eyes were darting back and forth from the wall, to his harness, to his mother and me, and then back to the wall. To say he was nervous about what he was about to do would have been an understatement.

After a deep breath he hesitantly turned to face the wall. Beginning at the very bottom he surveyed that mammoth structure in its entirety, tipping his head back to see clear to the very top. He took a moment to size up his own personal Goliath-size obstacle and then began to climb.

The first few movements came rather easily. But as he moved up the wall, the position of the rocks and blocks grew sometimes farther apart and more awkwardly placed. This meant Micah had to strategize and plan ahead where he wanted to place his foot and which handhold he would reach for next. As we hollered up to him cheers of encouragement, he would look over his shoulder for reassurance and for any guidance or strategic moves that might keep him moving. Spurred on by our cheers and applause, he seemed to gain more and more confidence the higher he climbed. He even looked over his shoulder less frequently.

When Micah finally reached the top of the rock wall, his face was positively beaming with exhilaration and pride in what he had just accomplished. You could see it all over him: "I did it!" Even from where we celebrated with him far below the platform, we could see a change in his physical posture. As he took in the view from his new perch, his shoulders were back and his chest was out, an involuntary external expression to the swelling pride and elation that was erupting like fireworks on the inside.

Even though I had been at the bottom of the wall the entire time Micah was climbing, ready to catch him if he happened to fall, through the strenuous process of the climb he exercised new muscles from fingers to toes that took him to new heights. When you go through a situation and release all the care, concern, and worry into God's lap, you are building spiritual confidence and climbing to new heights in God. "God can do it!" Though your situation might look like it's over, you might just be building new muscles and ascending a steep hill that will give way to an amazing view when you reach the top.

Don't Allow the Struggle to Immobilize You

Those few weeks in the hospital Josiah had to endure a very long and complicated surgery followed by several sessions of painful physical therapy. In fact, it was just shortly after surgery that the doctors and physical therapists came into his room to get him up and moving. Josiah was in such pain that the first goal given to Josiah by the therapist—to sit up in his bed for just a few seconds—brought on a flood of tears merely at the *thought* of moving. The incisions from Josiah's surgery, his spine, and the front and back of his neck were all so tender and sensitive that the slightest bit of movement elicited desperate cries from Josiah to "make it stop."

His therapist was incredibly kind and patient. She pulled my wife and me aside and very firmly stressed the importance of getting Josiah moving. She told us that as painful as it was for all of us, we had to let our son go through this process. She explained that the sooner Josiah got up and moving, the quicker his recovery would be. Josiah's level of surrender to this process now could make the difference in his recovery between a few weeks or a few months.

The words the physical therapists told us taught Jennette and me a valuable lesson and did give us a benchmark to work for. But watching our son fight through the crying, pain, and pressure his physical body had to endure was almost unbearable. In fact, there were several occasions during these therapy sessions that both Jennette and I had to excuse ourselves from the room because it became too difficult to sit there and watch Josiah fight through the trauma. When it became too much, we had to remind ourselves of her words, "The quicker Josiah is able to get out of bed and get his body moving, the quicker his wounds will heal and his strength will return." Though it seemed difficult, if Josiah didn't get moving, his healing would only be delayed. When you grab hold of a struggle and begin to *fight*, the quicker your strength and healing will arrive. You can't allow the struggle to immobilize you! You can't lie in bed and refuse to give your physical and spiritual muscles movement, however painful it might be.

I find it interesting that in the Bible boys were considered to be men at the age of thirteen. Jewish culture continues to honor this rite of passage with the celebration of the bar mitzvah. It is also worth noting that this is roughly the age some would consider to be the beginning of the age of accountability, the transition that occurs when a boy begins to take responsibility for his own actions. It was at this time that these boys would then set aside their games and toys and would instead begin to study and work as an apprentice. That is why Jesus was a carpenter. He was studying his father's trade. Though it is debatable and not exactly known, I believe Jesus's disciples were around the age of thirteen or fourteen.[2] They were studying under Him. It puts a whole different picture and understanding on biblical stories when you recognize the disciples could have been mere teenagers.

Today's generation is far from seeing our thirteen-year-olds as men. I'm not suggesting we throw our teens into the workforce and put them in their own apartments, but sociologists say we are living in a time of *extended adolescence*. At a time when, as adults, maturity should be present, there has been a lack of accepted responsibility and an enabling of our young men to continue playing games (oftentimes, literally!) instead of assuming responsibility for themselves and their actions.

These adults continue to behave as teenagers because they have not been equipped to handle and embrace struggle. They haven't allowed the fight of struggle to mature them in their behavior and thought patterns and thus still behave like high-school boys.

In many cases parents fail to offer their children the opportunity to face any challenges or to figure things out for themselves because the parents want to make life comfortable and easy for their children. I've heard it said so many times from parents to their children, "I worked hard, so you don't have to." When you take away the opportunity to allow your child to struggle, you take away the opportunity to allow your child to learn and grow. The struggle is where boys learn "manhood" and, for that matter, where girls learn "womanhood." There is a strength that comes when you learn to fight and take responsibility. As parents, or as children of God, you must put on the mantle of "grown-up believers" and embrace struggle as the opportunity to grow in your faith, grow in your determination, and grow in your witness to the world around you.

I'll break this open more in the next chapter, but the true strength of struggle is recognizing that the only fight you have is with your faith, your faith in the covenant God made with you and with me. As believers the outcome lies not in our own hands but in the hands of God. In Judges 6 the Bible talks about the story of Gideon. Let me paint a brief picture describing what it was like to be an Israelite like Gideon at that particular time. The Bible says the Israelites "did evil in the sight of the Lord" and worshiped the gods of the Amorites, so God handed them over to the Midianites. Now these people were so nasty and their dominance so oppressive—destroying crops, laying waste to the fields, and crowding the land with camels and tents—that the Israelites took to hiding in mountain caves to escape the torture. And when they just couldn't take it any longer, the Israelites cried out to God to help them. This is where Gideon entered the scene.

An angel of God was sent to inform Gideon that he had been chosen to free the people of Israel from the oppression of the Midianites. He was to start by removing the pagan idols from within the camp of Israel. The angel appeared to Gideon addressing him as "mighty warrior" (v. 11, NIV). That's quite a compliment from an angel of God—mighty warrior! For a man to bear that name he must have been brave of heart and fearsome in stature, right? Not in this case. The Bible says that Gideon was from Manasseh, the weakest tribe of the twelve tribes, and that Gideon was the runt of the liter (v. 15). In fact, when the angel delivered his message, Gideon was actually hiding away, doing his work in secret so he would not be found out and robbed by the Midianites. Gideon felt unqualified to handle the daunting task before him and was slightly dubious that the Lord was really on his side as the angel had declared. And although life under the oppressive hand of the Midianites was far from pleasant, the Israelites were very comfortable living their worldly pagan lifestyle and not really interested in change.

To allay his uncertainty Gideon requested of God, on three specific occasions, a confirmation that God had handpicked him for the task. He was so unsure of himself and insecure, he needed God to continually reassure him that he was doing exactly what God asked of him. Gideon said, "If you're serious about this, do me a favor: Give me a sign to back up what you're telling me" (v. 17, THE MESSAGE). It was almost as if Gideon was saying, "Listen, God, I really need to know this is You. Otherwise I'm going to get creamed by these people if You're not with me."

Isn't that how we talk to God sometimes? "God, if this is really You, please send me a sign." Gideon received confirmation after confirmation and decided to move forward with the assignment of leading an army to war. Gideon takes a small but well-selected army rightly chosen by God to go to battle with the Midianites and the Amalekites (v. 33). Gideon's army was whittled down to three hundred men, and the Bible says they were facing too many men to count.

> He [Gideon] divided the three hundred men into three companies. He gave each man a trumpet and an empty jar, with a torch in the jar. He said, "Watch me and do what I do. When I get to the edge of the camp, do exactly what I do. When I and those with me blow the trumpets, you also, all around the camp, blow your trumpets and shout, 'For GOD and for Gideon!'" Gideon and his hundred men got to the edge of the camp at the beginning of the middle watch, just after the sentries had been posted. They blew the trumpets, at the same time smashing the jars they carried. All three companies blew the trumpets and broke the jars. They held torches in their left hands and the trumpets in their right hands, ready to blow, and shouted, "A sword for GOD and for Gideon!"
>
> —JUDGES 7:16–20, THE MESSAGE

Now this is the part I really want you to see. Gideon gave each man an empty jar, a torch, and a trumpet. Three things.

God is so intentional in everything He does. As Gideon's army was facing what seemed to be an impossible situation, God had them take three things with them. Interestingly enough, three is the number symbolic of completion in the Bible. God is going to complete what He starts! The army was instructed to carry the empty jar, or earthen vessel as it is described by some translations, which represented humanity or man; the torch, which represented God; and the trumpet, which symbolized resurrection. As Gideon's army went into war, the army was instructed by Gideon to blow the trumpets and break their jars as the same time. Now picture this; the men carried their torches with the jar covering the flame and held their trumpets in their other hand. At the moment they faced their enemy, Gideon's army was instructed by God to break their jars, representing the breaking of their flesh. The breaking of their earthen jars exposed the flame from their torch, allowing the light of God to go before them. At that very moment Gideon and the men blew their trumpets, announcing resurrection or victory!

Isn't that exactly how it is with you and me at times? We feel, as was the case with Gideon, so unqualified or outnumbered, or, if we're willing to admit it, even forgotten by God. Our enemy or situation seems so much larger and stronger than the resources we possess in the natural. But God is calling you, just as He did Gideon, to break your flesh in the light of God's Word and blow the trumpet of victory, resurrecting newness of life and a changing of seasons. The strength that comes from watching God work on your behalf builds faith and pushes you to your next season.

The story of British Olympic runner Derek Redmond left

an indelible mark on society by demonstrating an undeniable tenacity to finish strong and embrace the struggle he faced.[3] Derek had trained his entire life to win an Olympic gold medal. Countless hours and intense workouts were spent with one goal in mind: to bring home a gold medal. Having had much success early in his career, winning medals in the 4x100 relay at the world and European championships and the Commonwealth Games, Derek was determined that his time for an Olympic medal would come at the 1988 Games in Seoul, South Korea. Much to his dismay Derek had to withdraw from the preliminary round of the 400-meter run just ninety seconds prior to his heat's scheduled start time due to an injury to his Achilles tendon.

Although Derek was immensely frustrated, he didn't allow the disappointment of this setback to discourage his goal. He would undergo a total of eight surgeries due to injuries, five of those in one year, resuming as soon as he was able to an intense training schedule with a gold medal in mind for the 1992 Barcelona Olympics Games. Derek endured the grueling physical workouts and intense mental focus required for an Olympian and was in perfect form by the time of his event.

Remembering the disappointment Derek had faced in the 1988 games, he was the favored contestant of the 65,000 fans in attendance on race day in Barcelona. His time was the fastest in the first round of the 400-meters, and he would win his heat in the quarterfinals. As the gun fired to signal the start of the semifinal race, the sprinters propelled into motion, each with the swiftness and agility only seen at this level of competition. Derek started the race well, but halfway through the back stretch coming into the final curve he pulled up suddenly and dropped to the ground. With a loud and practically simultaneous gasp the crowd stood to their feet in shock and disbelief. It was obvious that Derek was in excruciating pain. He had pulled his right hamstring muscle and was visibly crying out from the apparent intensity. In those few short seconds everything he had worked for vanished before his eyes. Derek's gold medal would not be waiting for him at the end. Some 200 meters down the track the race had ended and a winner declared, but all eyes were fixed on Derek.

Through tears and tremendous effort, Derek pulled himself to his feet, barely maintaining his balance on his one good leg, and began to hop toward the finish line. Life had thrown him a curveball, and he could have easily been assisted off the field that day and no one would have thought any less of him. He had given his best attempt but was now physically unable to complete the race. But Derek turned a sour situation into a tear-jerking display of strength in the midst of trial.

As Derek hopped toward the finish line determined to finish what he had started, his father fought his way through security to get to Derek's side, allowing Derek to lean on him as they limped toward to end. Derek knew that even though he had every right to quit, the moments of pain he endured while hopping were far less than the lifetime of pain he would feel by not finishing.

Sometimes your circumstances might feel like you are "hopping" through and barely limping along, but you build strength and create your testimony by embracing life's "it's not over" moments with confidence and your heavenly

Father's support. Even in the midst of a curveball, finish strong!

THE MARK OF STRUGGLE

When Josiah first came home from the hospital, we had a bed, oxygen tanks, and all of his medical needs set up downstairs in our master bedroom. Josiah was still being monitored on oxygen equipment at night and needed us nearby at all hours. I went to say his prayers one night, and he asked me to rub his back as a comfort to help him lull off to sleep. The room was dark in preparation for bed, and as I was gently rubbing Josiah's back, my fingers brushed across the top of his healing incision where the scar was starting forming from the stitches that ran vertically down the length of his neck. Initially I jerked my hand back

You know struggle will sometimes leave you marked. Genesis chapter 32 tells a story about twin brothers, Jacob and Esau. From the very moment of their birth, these brothers experienced much tension and fighting through the years. At this point in their story we learn that Jacob was hearing rumors that his bitter brother, Esau, was on the verge of attacking Jacob and his entire camp. As Jacob devised a plan to hopefully bring peace to his brother and safety to his belongings and family, he sent the majority of his caravan forward to flee from the suspected threat and then sat back and got some rest to clear his head and determine a plan. In the middle of the night an angel met Jacob, and the Bible says Jacob wrestled with this angel the entire night and would not let the angel go until he was blessed (vv.

24–26). Jacob fought in the spirit realm until he felt a release and received his blessing.

There are things you will have to fight and have the determination of Jacob to say, "I'm not letting go until you bless me." The fight of struggle, like Jacob's, will sometimes leave you marked. Genesis 32:25 says:

> When the man saw that he couldn't get the best of Jacob as they wrestled, he deliberately threw Jacob's hip out of joint.
>
> —THE MESSAGE

As I mentioned before, due to Josiah's surgery, Josiah has a very large scar down the front and back of his neck. Jennette and I told Josiah that the scar will forever be a reminder of God's faithfulness over his life. Josiah will always have a physical symbol, an outward reminder to himself and to others, that the hand of God covered and protected him when, in the natural, he easily should not be alive. Just as Jacob was marked by the angel of God, so Josiah can say he was marked by the hand of God.

KNOW YOUR NAME

While Jacob was wrestling with the angel, the angel asked Jacob, "What is your name?" (v. 27). His reply was, "Jacob." In the midst of struggle, you must know your name. If you don't know who are and what you believe, you will *not* receive the reward of the struggle. The Scripture says:

> The man said, "What's your name?" He answered, "Jacob." The man said, "But no longer. Your name is no

longer Jacob. From now on it's Israel (God Wrestler); you've wrestled with God and you've come through." Jacob asked, "And what's your name?" The man said, "Why do you want to know my name?" And then right then and there, he blessed him.

—THE MESSAGE

Jacob was facing an impossible situation. Esau stood to attack him and take everything he owned. Jacob was worried, concerned, and possibly even terrified. He did everything he knew to do in the natural, but it wasn't until he wrestled with the angel and was determined he wasn't letting go that he received his blessing. Sometimes struggle will mark you, but allow the marks to remind you of God's grace and catapult you to your next season. First Peter 4:12–13 says, "Friends, when life gets really difficult, don't jump to the conclusion that God isn't on the job. Instead, be glad that you are in the very thick of what Christ experienced. This is a spiritual refining process, with glory just around the corner" (THE MESSAGE).

4

THE VALLEY OF WHY

*"Where He leads me I will follow, I'll go
with Him, with Him all the way."*[1]

A FEW YEARS AGO I was rushing from my home church in Atlanta, Georgia, to catch a plane to be at another service for Sunday evening on the West Coast. A friend was driving me to the airport. We had only a small window of time to make the flight, so admittedly, we exceeded the speed limit a bit racing to catch my plane. If you've ever been to Atlanta, you're well aware that Atlanta traffic can be a little crazy. We were driving about eighty-five miles per hour down the interstate near Jimmy Carter Boulevard, which is a highly traveled, well-populated area. There is not much farmland or open space in the vicinity. We were driving in the fast lane, closest to the center median, which stood about six or seven feet tall.

Now picture this; the center median is separating the northbound and southbound traffic. I was traveling in the traffic heading south, so for something to cross the median, it first had to cross the oncoming northbound traffic. Both directions were well covered with vehicles, all traveling at sixty-five miles per hour or more.

My friend and I were laughing and completely oblivious to anything else outside the vehicle. All of the sudden, out of nowhere, a deer, yes, an actual deer, leaped the center median and came flying toward our truck! Please don't ask me how a deer made it across five lanes of traffic, leaped a center median, and was coming toward our vehicle. I have no idea where it came from. I have no idea how it got there or how it crossed all the other traffic. All I know is a deer jumped the median and hit our truck! Only by the grace of God were we OK. If the deer would have hit the car just a few inches higher, it could have come smashing through the windshield and, potentially, could have caused an extremely serious or lethal accident.

Isn't that just like life sometimes, though? You're driving along the road of life, laughing and having a good time, when all of the sudden, out of nowhere, a deer leaps the median and hits your car. Life can hit you out of nowhere.

When I received the phone call about Josiah, I was blindsided. Life was rolling along smooth and peaceful. But at that moment life left me asking why.

Admittedly one of the first thoughts that crossed my mind when I heard about Josiah's accident was "What?" and then,

"God, why? How could this happen to my son?" As natural human beings we simply cannot understand everything that occurs in our lives, both the good and the bad. But generally it's the bad things that leave us asking why. Some people spend their entire lives rooted in why. God, why this and why that? Having been a staff pastor at a few churches, I've spent hours with people who are struggling with the why, sometimes even decades after the event. The why in their lives has them stuck in that situation, unable to grow and move past their circumstances, still struggling with the confusion, hurt, brokenness, and emptiness left by pain or rejection. I've heard many times, "Why do bad things happen to good people?" Actually, bad things don't happen to good people; bad things can happen to *all* people.

Take, for example, Job. The Bible says he did everything right in the sight of God and shunned evil (Job 1:1). But Job was attacked in his health, in his family, and in his finances despite his righteous living. Job was actually a type and fore-shadowing of Jesus. The Bible says he was a righteous man, but disease, death, and devastation struck his life. Job was brought through the fire and, as you know, came out better on the other side. Life is not a respecter of people and will fall upon the just and the unjust. Matthew 5:45 says:

> To show that you are the children of your Father Who is in heaven; for He makes His sun rise on the wicked and on the good, and makes the rain fall upon the upright and the wrongdoers [alike].
>
> —AMP

Let me be perfectly clear. I do not believe God sends bad things your way to teach you a lesson. I said this in the previous chapter too. In fact, the Bible clearly states that the devil is the one who comes to steal, kill, and destroy (John 10:10). God is not the author of bad things. God is the author of all good things.

The word *devil* is interesting. If you actually break the word down, you will find that it is derived from the Latin word *diabolus*. *Dia* means "to break through" or to "pierce through," and *bolus* means "to continually cast at." The enemy's job is to continually cast accusation until he pierces through and keeps you from accomplishing your destiny. He wants to pierce your thought patterns and pierce through your faith. The enemy's job is to remind you of what someone said or did to you ten years ago, to remind you of your past and how others hurt you and failed to fulfill their promises to you. The enemy never gives up until he can break through your thoughts and you start believing the lies and actually think God is not for you. You can only justify it by saying, "Why else would all this *mess* be happening to me?"

FROM THE VALLEY TO VICTORY

There was a season after we returned home from the hospital when Josiah was having bad nightmares. He would wake up in the middle of the night crying, saying he was dreaming the accident was happening again, and he was scared to fall asleep. He would constantly ask, "Daddy, why did this have to happen to me? It just doesn't seem fair." Jennette and I spent a lot of time praying with Josiah and explaining that we can't control the circumstances in life, but we can control how we respond to the circumstances. We explained that though it seemed rough, it could have been much worse, and it's only by God's grace he was saved! Josiah is a walking, talking, and breathing miracle.

If you're not careful, life can make you take an easy detour and get caught in what I call the "Valley of Why." When you get stuck asking why all the time, you can end up living your entire life in the valley. Geographically, the valley is the low spot. If you are in the valley, you are at the lowest possible position, and you are at the bottom looking up. The valley can sometimes position you in the seat of being the victim. Oftentimes the valley is a state of mind. In the valley you're always feeling left behind, always taking the short end of life, assigning blame to other people, and offering excuses as to why you are the way you are. God didn't design for you to live in the valley looking up. Living in the valley of why can cause you to get stuck and never move into your full purpose.

Now please hear my heart; I'm not saying you should never ask why. Being instinctive, cognitive, and intelligent men and women of God will require that you internalize and investigate your life and life's issues. I'm referring to never being able to move on with your life because you are still holding on to the bitterness, brokenness, and hurt that materialized in your life from a situation that happened to you yesterday or years ago.

I'll never forget sitting in my office one day at a church that I worked for several years ago. As a shared responsibility all pastoral staff took a day of the week on which we rotated the duties of counseling and addressing church member's questions, concerns, or issues that needed to be discussed.

We referred to the role as POC, or pastor on call. I was in the office fulfilling my POC duties one day, and I remember having the receptionist buzz my assistant, saying there was a lady who urgently needed to see me. Normally drop-in appointments rarely worked with my schedule, but it just so happened that my previous appointment canceled, and I was free at that present time.

My assistant went and met the lady and escorted her to my office. As she sat down, I looked into her eyes that appeared to be well into their sixties and heard these words come out of her mouth, "Ricardo, I used to hate you. I hated you when you came on staff."

"Umm...have we met? Do I know you? How dare you walk into my office and say you hate me, especially without an appointment." All of this and a few other things went through my head as I sat there obviously stunned by her blunt and cold opening comments.

In all my years of ministry I've dealt with many things and even with unkind feedback, but I've never had anyone walk up to me and tell me they hated me. My disbelief obviously translated to my face because the woman continued by saying, "Let me explain. I was raised by an extremely prejudiced father, and I was trained to hate blacks, Hispanics, and all people that didn't look and act like me. My entire life was about hatred. I'd seen you lead worship many times, but at six five and with Caucasian skin color, I had no idea you were Hispanic until they introduced you as Ricardo Sanchez. It was then that I immediately felt this hatred toward you develop inside of me."

I felt a little relief knowing I hadn't intentionally done something to offend this lady. She simply hated who God made me to be. The woman continued with her story: "The hatred I had for different races began to overflow into every other area of my life. I hated everyone. When my dad passed away several years ago, I hated him and was angry about many things he had done to me. I began to ask God why he allowed so much hurt to affect my life. Why didn't God protect me? Why wasn't God there when I needed Him most? And then I realized I was allowing what my father did to me to still control my life many years later! I decided to take responsibility for my own actions and my own feelings. I didn't want my children to hate and continue the legacy of prejudice that my father had passed onto me. I forgave my father and instead of asking why, I decided to take what I've had to learn and help other people."

Wow. I sat stunned by the honesty and character it took to probably come and share everything I had just heard. But I knew this was also part of her healing. Like this sweet lady who had the boldness to visit my office that day, there are people who are allowing the whys in their lives to control their actions and thought patterns many years later. You might not ever have an explanation for the why in life, but you can control how you respond and move forward *after* the why.

I love the story of Mary, the mother of Jesus. She was a young girl, maybe twelve years old, when the angel of the Lord appeared to her and announced she would give birth to the Son of God. Having a child out of wedlock during that time was brutally shunned and the offender labeled and disregarded by society. Mary stood to lose everything. She easily could have said, "Why, God?" but her response in Luke 1:38 was, "Behold the handmaid of the Lord; be it unto me

according to thy Word. And the angel departed from her"
(KJV).

You might not know the purpose for the events in your life.
They might be unjust and they might be somebody else's fault,
but if you position yourself with the "be it unto me" attitude
and use *everything* in your life for the glory of God, you'll
move from the valley into victory.

TURN THE VALLEY OF WHY INTO WORSHIP

One thing that helped Jennette and I move from the valley
of why when evaluating the circumstances surrounding Josiah
and his accident was worship. Take a twist with me and picture the letter Y as a metaphor for the why in your own life.
Picture the Y as hands lifted to God in worship. Notice in the
picture below where the valley is located and where the abundant life is located.

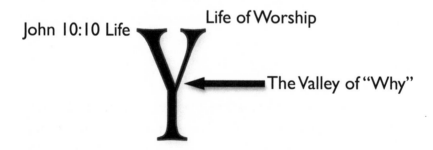

John 10:10 Life   Life of Worship

The Valley of "Why"

In order to stay out of the valley and spiritually on the
mountaintop, you must stay in a constant attitude of worship to experience the full life of John 10:10. Despite what
your situation looks like or what people may have said or done

to you, you must stay in an attitude of worship before God. Interestingly enough, if you look at the Y you'll notice there is a slope heading into the valley. A slope is easy to slide into and, because it's difficult to climb back out, it's easy to stay stuck in the valley. On the contrary, climbing up the slope is difficult and might require some effort. Be intentional with your life, your thoughts, and your words. Life's detours might not make sense, but God has a way of piecing the brokenness together. If you are in the midst of a situation that seems hopeless and you're not sure why you are going through it, lift your arms in worship and trust that though you don't see God at work, He is working on your behalf. Don't get stuck in the valley of why. Turn your why into worship.

That is the exact picture I get of the story in Exodus 17. The Israelites were in a battle against the Amalekites. The Bible says that Moses, Aaron, and Hur went to the top of the hill above the battle, and whenever Moses raised his hands, the Israelites were winning, but when his hands were down, the Amalekites were winning. When you are in a battle of why, you have to lift your hands in worship!

THE STINK ZONE

There are some people who have been in the valley of why so long it just seems normal. Sometimes you don't even know you're stuck in the why because you've been there so long. Have you ever heard of a stink zone? When I was a boy growing up in Arizona, it was my family's Sunday ritual to drive to an adjacent town about sixty miles west of Scottsdale to visit my grandmother in a town called Avondale. Avondale has since developed into a buzzing sub-metropolis of Phoenix, but back then it was an extremely rural and not very developed community with nothing but fields between the two cities. My grandparents, who spoke only Spanish, had settled there many years ago because of the year-round opportunity to pick lettuce and onions in the nearby fields, which was their livelihood.

Every Sunday my family of eight would pile into the station wagon and travel to Grandma's house for lunch and a family get-together. On our drive through the fields and rural crops, we would always hit this one section of town that stunk so foul and putrid we could hardly keep from plugging our noses when we stopped for snacks at the town's small gas station and convenience store. We couldn't understand how anyone could ever live with such a stench. My father would always say, "That is all these people know. They don't know it stinks because they've only lived here and don't know any better. How would they know it is supposed to smell any different?"

There are some people who have lived in the valley so long, they don't know anything different. They don't know what life can look like from the mountaintop of worship. The valley has become comfortable, but God did not design for you to live in the valley. God already went to the valley so you didn't have to.

Your situation may stink, but worship can change your perspective from the valley to the mountaintop. Your circumstance is temporal, but your worship is eternal. Ephesians 4:9–10 says:

> Is it not true that the One who climbed up also climbed down, down to the valley of earth? And the

One who climbed down is the One who climbed back up, up to the highest heaven. He handed out gifts above and below and filled heaven with his gifts.

—THE MESSAGE

Jesus climbed into the valley before ascending into heaven. You and I no longer need to live in the valley of despair, the valley of unforgiveness, or the valley of regret. We can lift our hands in worship because we know our risen Savior has all the answers we need. We may not understand the natural circumstances of life, but we serve a God who does, and we can rest in His provision and protection.

I want to address something I believe is a necessary issue to touch on briefly. My wife and I recently were talking with a dear friend who experienced betrayal in her marriage. This friend of ours made note of something I believe is a very real yet often unaddressed issue of the Christian life—feelings. Yes, it is true that you cannot allow your feelings to control you. However, not letting those feelings control you doesn't mean you deny those feelings exist. I think there is a religious voice that says, "Christians shouldn't have anger, hatred, disappointment." Christians shouldn't allow those feelings to *control* them, but it doesn't mean those feelings aren't present. You can't live with those emotions in your life, or they will eventually destroy you. But as you walk through life, you will experience emotions you must surrender to God and allow the work of the Holy Spirit to wash away the root and negative emotions. When you allow God to pull out the root, you will walk away with a testimony and a story that will pull someone else from their valley.

On the same subject of feelings, I'll never forget talking

with a family member who is very dear to my heart and who experienced both verbal and physical abuse and several affairs in her marriage before eventually deciding to file for a divorce from her husband of thirty years. Ten years after her divorce, she sat crying at the kitchen table during Thanksgiving one year saying, "Ricardo, I'm a Christian, but I can't get past the hatred. I wake up hating my ex-husband and everything he did to me. I know God doesn't want me to hate. What do I do?"

As people we have to process and work through the emotions that come with life's "it's not over" events. You must allow God to do a work in your heart. You are not a victim to your feelings. Just as we had to walk through the emotions with Josiah and how to handle the fear that wanted to control his life, so do you and I continually have to process how we handle the thoughts that develop from circumstances in life. Put your focus on God's Word, not on people, and your feelings will fall in line.

DIG A TRENCH

No matter what your feelings are telling you or how hung up on the why you are, you must do as Elijah says in 1 Kings 18:21: "How long will you waiver between two opinions? If the LORD is God, follow him; but if Baal is god, follow him" (NIV).

Now to set this passage of Scripture up, Elijah had announced several years prior that there was going to be a famine in the land. Ahab was king, and he and his forefathers were evil in the sight of God and worshiped the prophets of Baal. Elijah was nothing more than the mouthpiece for God, but to King Ahab, he symbolized the reason for the famine.

Elijah told Ahab to summon all the people and gather them together at Mount Carmel.

Elijah asked them, "How long will you be controlled by your feelings?" During that time Ahab's wife, Jezebel, was a zealous worshiper of Baal, who was the rain and fertility god. Though the Israelites were known to be worshipers of the One True God, many were converted to the pagan and idolatrous ceremonies of Baal. To put it in modern-day terms, Baal was popular. The king's wife, who had a platform of influence, openly participated in lavish acts of sensual worship in honor of the fertility god and swayed people by her position. There were Israelites who were moved by the ability to touch, see, and smell something they could put their faith in. They were moved by their *emotions*, not their *faith*.

Now this is my opinion: when things dry up and you're in a famine, just like the Israelites were, it is easy to be swayed by what you can see rather than what you know. You can't allow your feelings to dictate your actions just because you can *see* the results. You might feel anger, but if you act on your anger, you will reap a natural harvest. If you act on your bitterness, you will reap a natural harvest. The natural harvest of feelings is lustful and leaves you wanting more. When you act on the Word of God, you will reap a harvest birthed by the Spirit of God and produce a peace and assurance that you are not in control but God is.

So the Israelites and Baal worshipers gathered at Mount Carmel, and Elijah says in essence, "How long are you going to let your feelings control you? How long are you going to be swayed by what feels good at the moment? How long are you going to let your flesh control the situation?" And here is what Elijah proposed. He told every one of the four hundred fifty prophets of Baal to gather a bull to sacrifice on the altar and to call out to Baal to see if he would answer their cries. The prophets of Baal cried out all day and nothing. Nobody answered. There was no response. Then Elijah gathered everyone around him, and the Bible says he repaired the altar, which the Bible says had been torn down.

Elijah took what had been walked on and discarded. He took what was thrown away and treated as unimportant. He took what had been left for lost. He took what everyone else stopped putting value in and repaired it. He repaired the place where God would visit him and where he would visit God. Can you relate to what I'm talking about?

Maybe you're in a place where you need to repair the altar where you visit God and you allow God to visit you. Repair your prayer time. Repair your worship time. Repair the time you diligently seek Him. It's at the altar where your feelings get right. It's at the altar where your heart turns soft and you are able to hear the voice of God. Elijah repaired the altar that was torn down and put his sacrifice on the altar. The Bible says he dug a trench around his sacrifice and began to pour water on the altar:

> And he made a trench about the altar, as great as would contain two measures of seed. And he put the wood in order, and cut the bullock in pieces, and laid him on the wood, and said, Fill four barrels with water, and pour it on the burnt sacrifice, and on the wood. And he said, Do it the second time. And they did it the second time. And he said, Do it the third time. And they did it the third time. And the water

ran round about the altar; and he filled the trench also with water.

—1 Kings 18:32–35, kjv

I can only imagine what the Israelites where thinking. You have to remember that Elijah had the attention of the entire town. They are all out to watch the showdown between God and Baal. They all wanted to see who would answer. I'm sure there were many people who were thinking, "What in the world is he doing digging a trench? Why is Elijah wasting our time?"

What they didn't understand was that Elijah was being obedient. You might not understand some of the reasons you are doing what you are doing. You might not understand why you are having to "dig a trench" metaphorically speaking, but as you're digging, you're activating your obedience through *faith*. You might not understand why you have to pray, why you have to give, why you have to remain obedient, but as you're "digging your trench," you're preparing a place for the presence of God to come and sit around your offering!

I had no idea why I had to learn to sing when I was five years old. My parents weren't even believers. I was digging a trench. You might not understand why God has you serving in the children's ministry or why you are praying for a wayward child. You are digging a trench. You're preparing a place for God's anointing to come and fill your dry and barren land of famine. Dig a trench around and protect those things that God has asked you to consecrate to Him, and allow His anointing to fill your trench.

As a teenage boy one of my first jobs was working as a bag

boy at the local grocery store near my house. Being seventeen and working with other young men around the same age, it was apparent that most of the kids working at the store really wanted the money but very few really wanted to work. The most valued job amongst the employees was the one of collecting all of the shopping carts that gathered in the parking lot after customers loaded their groceries. We'd usually have to draw straws to see who would get to collect the carts on any given shift. This was a highly sought-after task because it was most of the employees' time to sneak in a hidden break.

My coworkers thought that because they were in the parking lot collecting carts, nobody would be looking or watching them, so they would meander in the parking lot, sneaking in a quick smoke behind a car or whatever they tried to disguise as work. Though I was your traditional teenager in many ways, I couldn't get past the thought, "What if my manager *is* watching? What if I worked like my manager was watching." And so my mantra became: "Work like your manager is watching."

When it would rotate to me to collect the shopping carts, I would *run* from cart to cart in the parking lot, gathering the carts as quickly as possibly and returning to my post inside or to assist wherever needed. After several months I was called into my manger's office. My manger said, "Ricardo, I've been watching the way you work. I appreciate your tenacity and diligence, and I would like to promote you."

When you're walking through a valley, it sometimes feels like God isn't watching, like nobody cares, but the valley is where you must diligently focus your efforts. God is not only watching over you, but He is also watching how you respond to the valley.

FIGHT THE FLESH

Waiting there in the terminal of the airport after receiving the news about my son, I was fighting my flesh—fighting the thoughts that my son would never walk again, fighting what the doctors were telling us. I felt like I was fighting something bigger than me. I was fighting my flesh when I heard the enemy tell me my son might have to breathe through a tube in his neck. I was in the valley, and the valley was trying to get in me. I had to fight the flesh.

I felt like the woman with the issue of blood must have felt in the Bible as she was frustrated by her condition and circumstances surrounding her, yet knowing that if she could just get to Jesus, she would be healed. As you may remember, this woman struggled with her flesh for twelve years and was unable to get better, though she visited a number of doctors. Mark 5:25–26 says:

> A woman who had suffered a condition of hemorrhaging for twelve years—a long succession of physicians had treated her, and treated her badly, taking all her money and leaving her worse off than before.
>
> —THE MESSAGE

It is obvious this lady was exhausted. Not only was she physically sick, but I'm guessing she was also mentally sick of people using her condition to better their cause and their pocketbooks. The doctors who were supposed to be helping her were taking advantage of her. They were taking her money but doing nothing to help her.

I love the picture I have in my mind of this woman. There was a crazy crowd of people around Jesus. People were pushing and fighting to get to the Savior. This lady had to fight through flesh *literally*, just to be able to touch Jesus. But she also had to fight the flesh *mentally*. She had to fight through the bad doctors' reports. She had to fight through the thought of all the money and resources she had exhausted, yet wasn't any better. And, I'm sure, she had to fight through family and their opinions and judgments about her dismal situation. I love that the woman with the issue of blood knew she just needed to get to Jesus. She knew she just needed to get to the Savior. Even in the crowd she had to literally fight through people to finally touch Jesus. Up to the very last minute she had to push "the flesh" aside to see Jesus. Her faith knew He was the only one who could heal her: "For she said, If I may touch but his clothes, I shall be whole. And straightway the fountain of her blood was dried up; and she felt in her body that she was healed of that plague" (Mark 5:28–29, KJV).

Flesh will always try and get in the way of you getting to Jesus. You must be determined to move the flesh aside in order to get to the virtue that flowed from heaven. When the woman with the issue of blood touched the hem of the Master's garment, Jesus said, "Who touched my clothes?" (v. 30, KJV).

Jesus will recognize and immediately acknowledge the touch of faith. The disciples were confused because so many people were touching Jesus, but the woman with the issue of blood touched Jesus with her faith, and virtue flowed from Him.

The valley can be a place where virtue flows if you push the flesh to the side and pursue Jesus with faith. Press in and don't allow the flesh of people or the flesh of what the world says to stop you from getting to the Savior.

When I was at the doctor recently for a checkup, my doctor mentioned one of the best and healthiest things to do for the body is to do an annual fast. Literally starve the flesh at least once a year to cleanse from the toxins and give your body and organs a break from the overeating. The flesh needs to be starved sometimes in order to see Jesus.

TURN YOUR *WHY* INTO YOUR *WINDOW*

Rather than stay in the valley of why and concern your life with the weight and pressure of the situation, turn your *why* into your *window*.

Genesis 37 introduces the story of Joseph and his journey from the pit to the palace. Early in the story we learn that Joseph had immediate favor upon his life that caused hatred to develop in his brothers' hearts toward him. Joseph was the youngest of his brothers and was his father's pride and joy. Joseph's brothers were working in the city of Dothan.

Interestingly enough, *Dothan*, by definition, means "two wells."[2] I believe "two wells" is symbolic of the two choices you have when life throws you a curveball. You can choose the "well" of bitterness and anger, or you can choose the "well" of life and surrender to God even though you may not understand the situation. Joseph's brothers plotted to kill Joseph and leave him for dead in a city that literally meant "two wells," and Joseph literally had to choose which "well" he was going to allow to manifest in his life.

Joseph didn't do anything to deserve being thrown into the pit and left for dead. Joseph couldn't have expected or anticipated the journey his life would take. The Bible says Joseph's brothers threw him into a cistern that was dry, literally with no water in it (Gen. 37:24). Have you ever been thrown into a symbolic dry, barren pit in your life? Being thrown into a pit in Dothan, I believe, is symbolic of Joseph's choice to turn his *why* into his *window*.

Joseph easily could have spent the remainder of his life sulking, wondering why his brothers were so mean to him, why his life was so unfair, and what he did to deserve such horrid treatment. He could have stayed in the place of wondering why God forsook him and left him to die. But he didn't mistake the dry, barren pit as a sign that God had forsaken him—and you shouldn't either. Sometimes the pit is about what you choose to do and how you react to the why. What you do with the why in your life can qualify you for victory or defeat. Joseph went from the pit in Dothan to the king's palace in Egypt. Pharaoh told Joseph:

> From now on, you're in charge of my affairs; all my people will report to you. Only as king will I be over you.
>
> —Genesis 41:40, The Message

Even though you might not understand your current season, you can turn it into a window of God's favor, blessing, and provision.

5

THE "NOT" SPOT

"Breathe on me, breath of God, fill me with life anew. That I may love what Thou dost love, and do what Thou wouldst do."[1]

'LL NEVER FORGET ministering at a church conference a few years ago for a pastor I hadn't met until the conference began. I was on the platform leading worship and was playing with a "house band," of sorts, that had been formed from musicians from around the country. I didn't have the comforts of my own team to lean on. I'll never forget, right in the middle of the second worship song, the power for the sound system went completely out. Nothing. No sound at all. The equipment that amplified what we were doing went silent. I'm not sure if you have ever been at a concert or even a church service when the power goes out, but it completely *stops* the flow and the environment you are trying to create, especially in a larger venue like the one mentioned above.

With no sound, I kept leading worship like nothing ever happened. Initially the band, as well as the congregation, looked stunned and a little bit like the adage "a deer in the headlights." But as I continued and moved on with worship, unaffected by the distraction, they too joined in, and we had a sweet time in God's presence. I found it interesting that after the service had ended, the other musicians came up to me and couldn't believe we didn't stop playing or even skip a beat when the sound cut out. I told the musicians what I tell musicians all across the country: that platform is a metaphor for life. What do you do when the sound cuts out in life? You keep going! You don't stop. You don't let it fluster you. You don't act awkward like it's a sign that you weren't supposed to be there in the first place. You don't throw a temper tantrum and yell at those around you. You keep moving forward! You have to move on and determine that there will be certain spots you are *not* going to stop on in your journey called life! Just like when the sound system cut out on me, there will be opportunities for you to stop *playing* when you are on the stage of life, but you must move forward unaffected by the distraction!

Most people get confused and think life is about what you see, but life is really conquered in the things you don't see. There are spots or snags throughout life where you will have to make internal choices that you are determined you are *not* going to stop and allow the circumstance to dictate your destiny. You are not going to get hung up on some of the snags that can trap your purpose. You must refuse to get stuck on what I call "the not spots" of life. The main "not spots" I've identified are heat seekers—bitterness, unforgiveness, and worry.

Inevitably there are always those questions and even pieces of "aftermath," if you will, from trials and "it's not over" circumstances that can leave a stench, a smell, a foul odor, or whatever you want to call it, that can emotionally cripple your purpose if not dealt with and dissected with God's Word. You have to have some issues settled in your heart and determine, "God, wherever You lead, I will follow!"

HEAT SEEKERS

No matter if you are on the mountaintop or in the valley, one of the spots you *cannot* stop on is "heat seekers." There will always be people who don't want you to change, who don't want you to grow, who have nothing positive to say about your future and where God is taking you. Sometimes these are the people closest to you—possibly even your family. Though they might have good intentions, they might not have God's intentions. These are the people I've come to call "heat seekers" and a "not spot" to avoid in the walk of life. Let me explain.

Several years ago I was at an outdoor shopping center in Scottsdale, Arizona. As I was walking from the parking lot into the complex, a beautiful black Mercedes drove in front of me. As the car rolled passed, I noticed one of the strangest sights I've ever seen. A snake was slithering out of the car's front hood. In disbelief my initial and gut reaction was to shout, "Hey, there's a snake coming out of your car!" hoping the driver would hear me. I had to shout a few times, getting louder with each time so the driver would stop.

Finally, my shout caught the diver's attention and the attention of those around us. He quickly threw his car into park and jumped out of the vehicle, leaving it idling in the middle of the crosswalk. All the commotion caused a small crowd to form around the reptile and the man's Mercedes. It seemed a bit dichotomous to have a rattlesnake slithering out of a luxury vehicle. One of the groundskeepers of the shopping center came over to assist and capture the four-foot long rattlesnake.

Afterward, as the three of us talked, I discovered that the groundskeeper was a long-time native of the Arizona desert and well versed in the habitat and lifestyle of reptiles. The owner of the vehicle asked the man why on earth would a rattlesnake be coming from his car, and the response was highly insightful. The groundskeeper said that reptiles, of any type, are unable to produce their own body heat. When temperatures drop, the animals must still find a way to stay warm and will seek external heat sources. This particular rattlesnake probably slithered underneath the car to lie on the engine to stay warm.

I've realized there are people in life who, just like the rattlesnake, are unable to reproduce their own heat and will try and seek out other people from whom they can steal heat. They are unable to find their own dreams, their own purpose, and their own vision. These same people always seem to be the doubters, those people who only look at the natural and are unable or unwilling to see the supernatural with hope and faith.

I read a story recently that I loved and perfectly describes the heat to which I'm referring.[2] A university professor was determined to undermine the Christian faith and those students who represented biblical truths in his class. He asked the class one day, "Did God create everything that exists?" One student bravely replied, "Yes, sir, He did. God created everything." Thinking he had the class on a one-way trip to his agnostic point, the professor continued, "Well, if God created everything, then God created evil. Evil exits, and according to the principle that our works define who we are, then God is evil."

The students became quiet before such an answer and were unable to respond to the professor's witting. The professor was pleased with his demonstration and was quite proud of his skills in instructing and boasted to the students that he had proven once again that the Christian faith was a myth.

A quiet class sat intimidated by the trickery, when another student raised his hand and said, "Professor, can I ask you a question?"

"Sure," replied the professor.

"Does cold exist?" asked the young man.

Almost belligerent the professor replied, "What kind of question is that? Of course cold exists. What a silly question. Have you never been cold?"

The other students snickered at the question and the bantering by the professor.

The young man replied, "In fact, sir, cold does not exist. According to the laws of physics, what we consider cold is merely the absence of heat. Everybody and every object is susceptible to study when it has or transmits energy, and heat is what makes a body or mass have or transmit energy. Absolute zero, -460 degrees Fahrenheit, is the total absence of heat. All matter becomes incapable of reaction at that temperature.

Cold, in fact, does not exist. *Cold* is a word we have used to describe how we feel if we have too little heat." The student continued as the professor sat perplexed, "Professor, does darkness exist?"

The professor replied, "Of course it does."

And the student replied, "Once again, you are wrong, sir. Darkness does not exist either. Darkness is in reality the absence of light. Light we can study, but not darkness. Darkness cannot be measured. Darkness is only measured by the amount of light that penetrates the darkness, and so I suggest it is with your theory of God being evil. Evil simply exists as the absence of God's presence. Evil is a word created to describe the absence of God's love present in your heart. God is not evil."

By definition of the laws of physics, *heat* is what makes a body have or transmit energy. When you spend time with God and pursue His plan for your life, you produce a heat that transmits into movement and direction. As you read above, cold is merely the absence of heat. Just as snakes are unable to produce their own heat, there are people who choose not to spend the time with their Maker and walk in a loving relationship with their Creator. You lose your heat, for lack of a better description, when you choose decisions that remove you from the presence of God and His direction on your life.

A person who has lost his heat is aimless, lost, negative, and oftentimes might describes themselves as "just being real." Haven't you ever met those people? You know the ones who say brutally honest comments not tempered with love and sensitivity, and they throw out the clause, "I'm just being real!" Usually those people who are "just being real" have no interest in growth and improving their own issues in life. They've become comfortable in stealing others' heat and are "being real" in order to lift themselves up and put others down. Heat seekers are people who have failed to pursue God on their own but desire the blessings of those who have. They are unwilling to spend the time with God to hear His voice and follow His direction for their own life. You must surround yourself with people of purpose and passion and not get stuck on relationships that aren't going to move you closer to God's plan for your life.

Saul in the Bible is such a perfect example of someone who lost his heat and who sought out external sources because he was unable reproduce his own, just like the rattlesnake. First Samuel 15 talks about Saul's kingship. Saul began his walk as a "nobody" and was truly humble before God. Samuel served as a priest and mentor over Saul's life, and Saul found strength in Samuel's wisdom and advice. Saul was truly anointed to serve as king and was sincere in his walk with God.

If you read in 1 Samuel 16:14, the Bible says, "At that very moment the Spirit of GOD left Saul and in its place a black mood sent by GOD settled on him" (THE MESSAGE). The spirit of the Lord departed from Saul because, if you read previously in 1 Samuel 15, Saul, through his own pride and arrogance, chose to remove himself from the presence of God's covering. God gave Saul very clear direction in 1 Samuel 15, and Saul was too proud to listen to God's direction. Listen to what 1 Samuel 15:12 says about Saul, "Saul's gone. He went to Carmel to set up a victory monument *in his own honor*" (THE MESSAGE, emphasis added).

Saul lost his own heat the very moment he decided he

should get the glory instead of God, who anointed him king in the first place. God has a plan that is specific for you, and you alone. You must spend the time with God and exercise disciplined efforts to keep your own "heat" alive, and avoid those people who are looking to *borrow* your purpose and the anointing on your life and ultimately will drain your energy.

In identifying heat seekers in your life, you must be aware that those people may manifest in a variety of different ways. I'll never forget what happened a few years ago after a service one day at a church I worked for. The church happened to be in a part of the country where, unfortunately, racism was still an issue. After leading worship, I was standing around talking with a few people in the church when I noticed a lady standing nearby waiting to talk to me. I made myself available, and I will never forget what she said: "Ricardo, you just need to get on your *burro* and go back to Mexico!" Wow. I was shocked. "Are you kidding me?" I was thinking. I was dumbfounded that it was 2005 and someone had the audacity to speak such vile, hateful words.

You know the Bible says in Matthew 12:34, "For out of the abundance of the heart the mouth speaks." People will call you by what they see or by what they think, but Jesus will always call you by your destiny! Your enemy knows your name but calls you by your weakness. God knows your weakness and calls you by your name. You can't allow people's words or actions to cause you to stop moving forward. You must realize people are not your source; neither are they your answer. Your destiny doesn't lie in the hands of people; your destiny lies in the hand of God.

TOO BLESSED TO BE BITTER

Have you ever sat down to eat what looked like an amazing meal and taken a bite of vegetables that looked tantalizing, but after you bit into them, you realized there was a bitter piece that left you looking for a trash can to spit into? Bitterness leaves an aftertaste that is unpleasant and lingering. You almost have to eat something else to wash away the bitter taste if you've ever eaten anything bitter. So it is with life. Bitterness is lingering, unpleasant, and leaves a horrible aftertaste in the mouths of those you encounter and, again, is a "not spot" of the Christian life.

"Sure, Ricardo, it's easy for you to say. Your son is alive and walking. Your story turned out to be a miracle." I recognize you may have walked through trials and have come through on the other side with results not ending quite like you pictured. Maybe you thought you would be farther along in life than you are currently. Maybe you never thought you would have to deal with some of the issues and mess that have come your way. Maybe you thought you'd be married by now, or maybe you thought your marriage would have never ended. The tendency in life, when you suffer difficulty, is to walk away with bitterness or anger at the longsuffering you endured. In fact, one of the definitions of bitterness is *marked by resentment or cynicism*.[3] Resentful of where you are, resentful of the loss you've endured, resentful of people who have treated you wrong, resentful of situations that seem unfair... the list could go on and on.

There has to be an intentional, determined mind-set to address and release bitterness, intentionality toward the mantra "Too blessed to be bitter." To focus on the issue, the problem, or the wrongdoing will only provide "crawlspace" for bitterness to breed. Bitterness is an emotion that will enlarge when given the space and will grow into hatred, a hard heart, and a closed door to the things of God. What you focus on will grow.

I heard a statistic recently that was so interesting to me. A well-known weight-loss company was airing ads on the radio to solicit business, and they said that the average weight gain over the holidays, from Thanksgiving through the New Year, is only one pound! I was shocked. That commercial went on to say, "It's the mind-set that people have over the holidays." The mind-set is to gain weight, so people think they have gained more than they truly have. The mind-set grows and gives you the impression you've gained a surplus of weight. Bitterness is the same way. It's a mind-set that will grow and affect how you think, how you process, and how you interact with people.

Let me show you something that blew me away when reading the Bible. I'm sure you are familiar with the Passover ceremony when the angel of death would see the blood of the lamb on the doorposts and literally *pass over* the Israelites' house. But have you ever connected the Passover to bitterness? Let me show you what God showed me recently. Read Exodus 12:1 when the initial instruction for the Passover is given:

> Now the LORD spoke to Moses and Aaron *in* the land of Egypt…
>
> —EMPHASIS ADDED

God spoke to Moses and Aaron while they were still *in* Egypt. God spoke while they were still in their bondage, while they were still held captive by their oppressor. Do you know how brutal the Israelites were treated while in Egypt? The Israelites were the slave dogs. They were the grunt workers. They were at the beck and call of the Egyptians and were treated with indignation, disregard, and abuse. But God spoke to them while they were still in the middle of the bondage and spoke to them about their freedom and about the release of any bitterness they may want to take with them from their bondage. "Bitterness?" you say. "I don't remember it talking about bitterness." Let me show you.

During biblical times the hyssop plant was used to cleanse. It was symbolic of a detergent, if you will, and was often used to clean sacred places, such as the temples. In fact, you can read scripture after scripture in the Bible where it references being cleansed with hyssop. Read what David wrote in Psalm 51:7: "Purge me with hyssop, and I shall be clean; wash me, and I shall be whiter than snow."

The hyssop plant is known to be an odorless root but to have a bitter, nauseous, somewhat acrid taste. Now follow me. If you were to simply smell the plant, you wouldn't notice anything odd. It's not until you bite into the root that you would want to spit it back out! That's how bitter people are. You wouldn't notice it by looking at them, but once you bite in, metaphorically, you open up a bitter, nauseating taste.

This is what the Israelites were instructed to do with the hyssop:

> And you shall take a bunch of hyssop, dip it in the blood that is in the basin, and strike the lintel and the two doorposts with the blood that is in the basin.

And none of you shall go out of the door of his house
until morning.

—Exodus 12:22

The Israelites were instructed to take their bitter root and dip it into the blood of the lamb and paint it over their doorposts. You have to take those bitter things and bitter roots in your life and dip them into the blood of the Lamb and wash them in the blood that was shed on the cross of Calvary for you and for me. Only the blood of Jesus can cleanse bitterness. You have to dunk your bitter feeling in the blood. It is only by the blood you can release bitterness. You have to leave it at the cross. Remember, once the Israelites painted their doorposts, the angel of death would pass over their house. When you leave bitterness dipped into the blood of Jesus, the death angel will pass over your life. It might be the death of your will. It might be the death of your pride. It might be the death of your own agenda, but the death angel will pass over when the blood is present. The blood will cleanse the "not spot" of bitterness.

Did you know God actually instructed the Israelites as to *how* they were to eat their Passover meal? Look what Exodus 12:11 says:

And here is how you are to eat it: Be fully dressed with your sandals on and your stick in your hand. Eat in a hurry; it's the Passover to GoD.

—The Message

Why in the world would God take the time to instruct the Israelites to eat fully dressed, with their shoes on, and their keys in their hand? They had to be ready to go. This wasn't a "kick back and stay awhile" meal. They were prepared to move at the very Word of God. Basically, the bitter root was to remain in the blood, and the Israelites were to be prepared to move from bondage into freedom at a moment's notice. God does not want you stuck in bondage with bitterness hanging over your house. Though the Old Testament is just a picture of what was provided in the new covenant, the law and sacrificial order give us a clear and distinct picture of exactly what and how God wants His children to live—free from oppression, both spiritually and emotionally.

Bitterness is a root that can grow and deepen until it has destroyed the vessel in which it is rooted. Read what Hebrews 12:14–15 says:

> Work at getting along with each other and with God. Otherwise you'll never get so much as a glimpse of God. Make sure no one gets left out of God's generosity. Keep a sharp eye out for *weeds of bitter discontent*. A thistle or two gone to seed can ruin a whole garden in no time.
>
> —THE MESSAGE, EMPHASIS ADDED

Michal, one of David's wives, was watching one day as he was bringing the ark of the covenant back into the city. She was watching from a window, looking down onto the street as David was dancing before the Lord and the ark of the covenant and all the people, and the Bible says, "She despised him in her heart" (2 Sam. 6:16). Bitterness will set in when you sit back from afar and watch the things of God, judging rather than participating.

Michal was Saul's daughter and had been around the ark of the covenant her whole life. She was familiar with the presence of God, possibly too familiar. Michal knew all about it, but she lacked the intimacy David had with the Lord that allowed him to openly dance before Him without a concern of what people thought. Just like Michal, looking from a window above David, you can be sure bitterness has taken root when you look down on others around you. Bitterness judges and condemns.

I find it interesting that Michal was given to David to be his wife right after he finished one of his greatest battles and defeated the giant Goliath. The whole country was high on David and sang and shouted his praises. The Bible says in 1 Samuel 18:28 that when Michal was given to David in marriage, she loved him very much. As a side note in fact, the Bible goes on to say that this is the point when Saul initially realizes how much favor is on David and recognizes how much his own daughter loves David. You can see the hatred begin to settle in Saul's heart.

But what happened between 1 Samuel 18 and 2 Samuel 6 when Michal went from loving David to despising David? What happened from a soft tender spirit to a hard, judgmental woman looking detestably through a window at her husband? Life happened. Whatever it was—whether it was the pressure from her family because her father despised David or if she felt neglected as David continued to develop a friendship with her brother Jonathan—somewhere along the way Michal stopped on the spot of bitterness and allowed it take root in her heart. The bitterness grew into hatred, and the hatred ultimately kept her from participating actively in worship before

God. She became critical and probably began to process life with comments like, "Yeah, I've seen that before" or maybe "You should see what David is like at home." Whatever the reason, she held wrongdoings in her heart that made her hard.

Michal proves to be a great example of why it's important to protect your heart from the bitterness that tries to take root through life's "it's not over" moments.

SHUN THE "UN"

In 2007 I cowrote a song titled "I Am Forgiven." I'll never forget one of the first times I sang the song in a church setting. The chorus of the song goes like this:

> I am forgiven
> I have been given another chance
> No condemnation
> Your grace is sufficient to cover my past
> Your love is more than enough
> More than enough for me.[4]

I was singing this song during the altar call, which was given following a powerful message. A man who looked as if he had lived a hard life responded. There were probably a few hundred people who responded to God that day, but it just so happened this man was standing right in front of me in relation to where I was on the platform. I could hear the man shout out to God, "God, can You really forgive me? God, do You know what I've done?" Because the music was playing, nobody could really hear him but me. His sincerity and desperation touched my heart. You could see he was truly looking for answers, but he couldn't get past the thought that God couldn't forgive someone who lived a life less than perfect.

The Bible says in Ephesians 4:32: "And be ye kind one to another, tenderhearted, forgiving one another, even as God for Christ's sake hath forgiven you" (KJV).

Before we even address the issue of "shun the un," we must first settle this issue: no matter what you have done in life, nothing is beyond the reach of Christ's love and forgiveness. No sin is too heinous or too bad that you can't bring it to the cross and receive love, acceptance, and forgiveness. What Jesus did on the cross is done. That same generosity of forgiveness that God has extended to us as believers is to be extended to those people in life who offend and wrong you. "Wait a second, Ricardo. You have no idea what they did to me." No I don't, but forgive them.

Sounds easy enough, but when people do things or life happens, forgiveness sometimes is easier said than done. However, unforgiveness will rot and cripple your relationships with other people and with God. I've heard it said that harboring unforgiveness is like drinking poison and expecting the other person to die. Choosing not to forgive is trying to tell the offender, "I want you to hurt as badly as you made me hurt."

Unforgiveness is a not spot and really should be regarded as one of the most dangerous emotions to harbor. Unforgiveness is the root from which bitterness and anger spring and can oftentimes be recognized with certain thought patterns that you must intentionally arrest at the moment they try and rear their ugly heads.

You may not know it, but you wear unforgiveness on your face. You wear unforgiveness in actions and your attitudes toward other people. The Bible says in Proverbs 23:7, "As he thinks in his heart, so is he." Have you ever noticed that unforgiveness forces you to sometimes go where you may not want to go? Unforgiveness can actually control your life. "What are you talking about, Ricardo?" you might be saying. "I do what I want. I'm not controlled by unforgiveness."

Let me explain with a story. My parents got divorced after thirty-two years of marriage. Though I was an adult when they finally divorced, there was a tremendous amount of family issues that had built up through the years. Resentment, unforgiveness, and anger were just a few of the emotions welling up in my life at that time. I would avoid going to certain weddings, birthday parties, or events if I knew certain family members were going to be there because of the unforgiveness in my heart. The unforgiveness, whether I would have admitted it at the time or not, made choices for me and withdrew me from spending time with the people I loved.

After I had met Jennette and we had become engaged to be married, I knew I didn't want to carry the same emotional patterns into my life with her and our new beginning together. We were getting ready to create our own family, and I wanted to start with a clean slate. Through the process of my parents' divorce, there were several things that opened the door for me to hold unforgiveness in my own heart toward my father. I hadn't spoken to my father in over three years. There was a lot of anger and hurt toward my dad through the divorce and from years before. Even though I was an adult, the pain and hurt affected me in a deep way. I didn't want to give that root of unforgiveness a foothold or any opportunity to breed in the family I knew Jennette and I would one day start.

Little did I know at the time, God was going to give me three sons of my own. All along I was the so-called "Christian," yet I was waiting for my father to initiate reconciliation. I remember feeling the Holy Spirit's nudge to make things right with my dad. I was sitting in the basement of a friend's house and I rang my father. My dad answered the phone and said the words, "Hi, son." I immediately broke into tears. I hadn't been called "son" in over three years, and the emotions of unforgiveness I had been holding shattered on the phone that day. I wept with my father and asked him to forgive me for actions and attitudes that I had done to wrong him. I realized that it was my pride that kept me from calling my father sooner because I didn't think I had done anything wrong. I was expecting my father to come to me, but the lesson I learned was this: the release of forgiveness, whether you think you are right or wrong, will open the doors of favor and blessing over your life and over household.

What would happen if you chose to forgive someone you've been holding resentment against? What would happen if you picked up the phone right now and made a phone call and released forgiveness to someone on the other end of the line? Forgiveness can be scary. Forgiveness can be vulnerable. Forgiveness or unforgiveness can extend beyond generations. What if you broke the cycle for your family and offered forgiveness?

WORRY WASTE

I would be lying to you if I said that men don't worry, but in general and according to a nationwide survey, it's been found that women worry nearly twice as much as men, with financial worry being the greatest concern of all.[5] After a quick consultation with my wife, I've learned that women can worry about everything from paying bills on time, to their kids' future, to uncertainty in relationships, to the newest strain of deadly diseases put out by the CDC, to approaching deadlines, rising gas prices, world hunger...the list goes on and on.

Worry and fear can control and govern your thought process and interfere with how you view God and interface with His promises. Worry is relentless and, just like bitterness, will continue to grow and dominate your thoughts until arrested.

Proverbs 12:25 says, "Worry weighs us down; a cheerful word picks us up" (THE MESSAGE). Worry weighs you down. Worry makes you heavier. Worry makes life burdensome. Worry is a "not spot" of life and can only be snuffed out when you choose to feast on the Word of God and not what CNN is saying. God never intended for you to worry. Worry is a manifestation of a lack of trust in God and who He is. If you truly believed what His Word said, why would there ever be a need to worry. God has it under control!

> Can all your worries add a single moment to your life? And why worry about your clothing? Look at the lilies of the field and how they grow. They didn't work or make their clothing, yet Solomon in all his glory was not dressed as beautifully as they are. And

if God cares so wonderfully for wildflowers that are here today and thrown into the fire tomorrow, he will certainly care for you. Why do you have so little faith? So don't worry about these things.

—MATTHEW 6:27–31, NLT

Worry is waste—wasted time, energy, and emotions. Nothing is ever accomplished by worrying. First Peter 5:7 says, "Give all your worries to God, for he cares about you" (NLT).

Worry will wear you out! It's exhausting to worry, and the irony is this—worry does absolutely nothing to change your circumstances. I recently read a statistic by an online British publication put out in 2008 that said, on average, "Women will spend seven years and ten days stressing, while men will spend five years, eight months, and 23 days."[6] What a waste of time! Don't waste your time on worry, but instead trust that God is at work.

6

BEAUTY FOR ASHES—THE EXCHANGE

*"Mercy is calling you, won't you give heed? Must
the dear Savior still tenderly plead? Risk not
your soul, it is precious indeed; what would
you give in exchange for your soul?"*[1]

A FEW YEARS AGO Jennette and I were having a date
night, and we had the opportunity to attend an event
in downtown Atlanta at the infamous Fox Theatre.
The event was a dressy occasion. People were wearing their fur
coats, and a few men were dressed in tuxedos. I was feeling
rather debonair at my selection to treat my wife to a nice night
out and was looking forward to a great concert. If you've ever
been to the Fox Theatre, you know you have to park and make
your way into the box office and ticket area. At the time we
had just released our second live worship record, and we were

receiving some national and international recognition as a songwriter and worship leader. I could hear people whispering as we walked along, "That's Ricardo Sanchez." "Oh my gosh! That's the worship leader Ricardo." Admittedly, I began to walk with a new swagger, if you will. "Yeah, baby, you're with *the man* tonight," I began to whisper into Jennette's ear. She would look at me and roll her eyes as if to say, "Really? You're really going to call yourself *the man*?"

The night continued, and the concert was incredible. At intermission Jennette and I went to get some snacks, and several people stopped me to ask for my autograph. "Oh yeah! You are *definitely* with *the man*. How does it feel to be married to *the man*?" I continued to tease, but "the man" comments persisted to remain the central theme and joke for the evening.

After the show Jennette and I were walking on the sidewalk to head back to our car, and a group of people from across the street shouted, "Hi, Ricardo! We love your music!" "Wow, you must be the luckiest girl in the world to be married to 'the man.' Baby, God must love you," I said with a smile and a wink.

Another group was walking, and I heard them shouting and running toward us, "Ricardo! Ricardo!" I could hear from behind. I turned around to see one of the girls grabbing her camera. I was now getting a little exhausted with all the fanfare, for lack of a better description, and the joke seemed to be wearing a little thin with Jennette. As the lady was getting closer to Jennette and me, she said, "Ricardo, will you take a picture?" As I was walking to join the group so they could have a picture of "the man," I noticed the lady was handing *ME* the camera so I could *take* their picture! They didn't want me to be *in* the picture; they just wanted me to *take* their picture. As I went to grab the camera, I caught Jennette looking at me with a smile as she whispered under her breath, "Baby, remember, you're *the man!*" Needless to say, I stopped joking about being "the man."

After eating my dose of humble pie, I was reminded that in life's victories and in life's defeats, at the end of the day, it has very little to do with me. It's all about God! It's easy to get things confused and think it has something to do with you or me when, in essence, it has nothing to do with us. It's all about the beautiful exchange Jesus made for us on Calvary, when He took our ashes and made something beautiful by His blood.

Though some parts were in jest, I hope this story conveyed and illustrated the point that your purpose and your destiny in life are contingent upon one thing and one thing alone— the exchange Jesus Christ made for you at Calvary. He took everything we deserved to the point of death and in exchange established a covenant between man and God. I understand people need a point of contact and are able to connect with humanity and funny stories as examples, but we, as human vessels, are nothing more than that: simple vessels. Who we are and what we do is nothing without the exchange Jesus made for us.

Little did I know that when I cowrote and recorded the title cut for the album *It's Not Over* that my family and I would actually get to live out the testimony of the song with Josiah. God had given me these lyrics months before Josiah's accident. Now I know with all my heart that God foreseeably provided me with this song, knowing full well that I would be ιg them over my son in his hospital bed. I truly believe this God-ordained song was given to me as a way to minister first to our spirits, my family's and mine, before I would share it with others. The richness of the song cemented its way through our tragedy, through our victory.

IT's NOT OVER

I know it's dark just before dawn
This might be the hardest season you've experienced
I know it hurts
It won't be too long
You're closer than you think you are
You're closer than you've been before
Something is moving, turning around
Seasons are changing, everything is different now
Here comes the sun, piercing the clouds
You're closer than you think you are
You're closer than you've been before
It's not over, it's not finished
It's not ending, it's only the beginning
When God is in it
All things are new.[2]

Walking through this situation with Josiah has solidified our foundation, even as parents, and has reinforced our motives to be very intentional in how we "do life" and how we raise our sons. It has made me quite reflective on my life as a believer in Jesus Christ. My wife and I have always been very deliberate in the way we have raised our boys—to be men of God, to be men of God's Word, and to be men true to their word. Nevertheless, since Josiah's accident, we purposefully wanted them, as well as ourselves, to know and understand their covenant with God, their relationship with God, and our foundation as children of God.

God's Word, an Eastern book in our Western culture, gives us many word pictures or analogies about our relationship with God:

- He is the Shepherd—we are the sheep.

- He is the Father—we are the children.

- He is the Potter—we are the clay.

- He is the Head—we are the body.

- He is the Commander—we are the army.

- He is the Master—we are the servants.

Each of these images provides us with clear directives on how to live out our covenant relationship. Yes, it is God's responsibility to provide for our needs, to teach and guide us, to help us move forward and prevail, and to establish our portion. And in that we must trust and believe.

Society today has a hard time understanding the true weight of a biblical covenant because in today's climate contracts, promises, and covenants are easily broken, annulled, and voided all the time. Our present age is one of shattered promises and broken relationships. This age has lost sight of the fundamental pledge "till death do us part." A covenant is an endless and binding partnership between two or more parties. Our covenant with God provides a commitment to a relationship that allows His purpose for us to be fulfilled.

In the book *The Covenants*, Kevin Conner and Ken Malmin define covenant this way:

> The word "covenant" is a word that has lost its meaning and significance in present day. In Bible times, the word "covenant" involved promise, commitment, faithfulness and loyalty even unto death. A covenant was sacred and was not lightly entered into by the parties involved. In Bible times, a person was only as good as their covenant word. In a society where national agreements, business contracts, and marriage covenants are under stress and attack, where people are "covenant-breakers" (Romans 1:31), it brings great joy and comfort to know that God is a covenant making and covenant keeping God.[3]

Therefore, every one of us who has experienced the amazing and saving grace of God has entered into a covenant agreement with Him—the new and everlasting covenant. This is not just some abstract promise of everlasting life, but it is a personal and very real covenant. Our covenant with God is His plan for our blessing; it's our inheritance. However, for us to possess this, we must understand fully our responsibility and our agreement to God, our part of the covenant.

Before the Fall God expressed His purpose for mankind in Genesis 1 and 2 as being made in God's image, being fruitful and multiplying, having dominion, and so on. When Adam and Eve broke their part of the covenant with God in Genesis 3, God's redemptive purpose for the human race was propitiated. After this point we see God establish a series of redemptive covenants with us as humans—with Noah (Gen. 6–9), with Abraham (Gen. 12–22), with Moses on Sinai (Exod. 19–40), with Phineas (Num. 25:10–13), with Israel (Deut. 27–33), with David (2 Sam. 7; Ps. 89; Ps. 132), and finally, with His new covenant in Jesus Christ (Jer. 31:31–34; Matt. 26; Heb. 8). What amazing and overwhelming promises!

The first time that the Bible actually uses the word *covenant* is in Genesis 6:18. God created a covenant with Noah that has affected our world ever since—it really has messed up science today! I think that the very meaning of Noah's name, which is "rest," really solidifies God's prophetic purpose for a man He knew would obey and trust Him. The people of that day had strayed so much in sin and away from God's plan that He literally had to start over. And it was in Genesis 9:8–11 that God gives a covenantal blessing and a way for us to remember His promise—the rainbow:

> Then God said to Noah and to his sons with him: "I now establish my covenant with you and with your descendants after you and with every living creature that was with you—the birds, the livestock and all the wild animals, all those that came out of the ark with you—every living creature on earth. I establish my covenant with you: Never again will all life be cut off by the waters of a flood; never again will there be a flood to destroy the earth."
>
> —NIV

Yet the Bible shows us that it was God's sovereign plan to establish His covenant through Abraham—or Abram, as he was originally named. God's promises to Abraham can be summed up in Genesis 12:2–3, which is a sevenfold structure:

1. I will make you a great nation.

2. I will bless you.

3. I will make your name great.

4. You will be a blessing.

5. I will bless those who bless you.

6. Whoever curses you, I will curse.

7. All peoples on earth will be blessed through you.

The Abrahamic covenant really solidifies our human intent, restores mankind's original blessing, and extends us as seeds of "our father Abraham," the first man to be called a Hebrew. God said to Abraham in Genesis 17:7 that He is "establishing my covenant between me and you, a covenant that includes your descendants, a covenant that goes on and on, a covenant that commits me to be your God and the God of your descendants" (THE MESSAGE).

Because Abraham was a Semite, a descendent of Noah's son Shem, all Jews trace their ancestry to him as the father of the Hebrew nation. (See Genesis 11:10–32; 14:13.) Peter reminds the Jewish believers in Acts 3:25 that they are heirs of the covenant God made with Abraham. But it is Paul who tells the Gentile believers that all Christians find their origin in Abraham: "If you are Christ's, then you are Abraham's seed" (Gal. 3:29). Therefore, the biblical phrase "our father Abraham" (John 8:53; Acts 7:2) expresses the family relationship that every person of faith has with "the man of faith." (See Galatians 3:9.) What a promise; what a heritage; what a responsibility!

Not long ago America became intrigued with family trees or genealogy. Movies and documentaries such as *Roots* triggered such an interest with people. It seems to have started a craze in America for people to begin tracing family, ethnic, and national ties. This is all well and good, but at the same time, many Christians have little to no knowledge of their biblical roots and thus their covenant commitment.

In order to understand our commitment as believers, it is important to fully grasp the magnitude of covenant or the exchange God made with Abraham. This intense process of what both parties go through truly demonstrates and exemplifies how permanent and binding a covenant was and is. It also expounds upon how God anticipates His relationship with us to be. In a covenant the weaker or less endowed party actually assumes and receives the benefits of the greater, wealthier party. The covenant was for life and was a binding act between two individuals. A biblical blood covenant could never be broken.

The covenant is the reason and the hope you and I hold when we face an "it's not over" moment in life. Covenant was to give man a hold upon God as the covenant-keeping God, to link him to God Himself in expectation and hope. Thus covenant is the basis from which we must act and react. Being so engrained in us, our covenant with God must completely determine the position from which we make all of our decisions. In order to totally get the full picture of what God was saying when He established His covenant, we must understand the nine-step process involved in the biblical covenant. This is how serious God is about His promises, His covenant. As you read the nine steps below, truly absorb the weight of

God's promises in light of the exchange made between God and Abraham's seed, or you and me.

STEP 1: THE EXCHANGE OF ROBES OR GARMENTS

During Hebrew times the robes or garments people wore were symbolic of a person's status in life. Kings or priests wore royal garments, symbolizing their authority and their kingship—as seen in Esther 6:6–9 when Haman makes a fateful request to wear the Persian king's robe and parade through the street. By symbolically exchanging robes, a person initiated the act of saying, "Everything I have is yours, and everything you have is mine. Everything I have access to, you have access to." It can be viewed as taking off the "old self" and putting on a "new self. This new relationship heralds an end of independent living for both parties involved since they are now called to live for each other. There is to be a surrender of self-interest for the covenant partners.

First Samuel 18:3–4 is a prime example of this exchange of robes between David and Jonathan. This powerful exchange, initiated by Jonathan, appears to involve a pledge of loyalty and friendship. At the very least Jonathan accepts David as his equal:

> And Jonathan made a covenant with David because he loved him as himself. Jonathan took off the robe he was wearing and gave it to David, along with his tunic, and even his sword, his bow and his belt.
>
> —NIV

While David, the simple shepherd boy, puts on the prince's robe and garment, Jonathan, King Saul's son, acts in a way of honor, equality, and vulnerability as he stands humbly in, quite possibly, his undergarments. Jonathan demonstrates his commitment to this solemn covenant by giving David his royal robe. Wearing the robe of the prince or possibly the future king was not only an immense honor but was completely prophetic in this exchange.

Jonathan's figurative act formally eliminated David's status as a shepherd and placed him side by side as an equal. His disrobing was a conscious display of vulnerability and utter risk in saying, "My life for your life." As this practice was completely understood in biblical times, in a symbolic sense and in the context of covenant, David is "putting on" Jonathan. David is taking on the identity of his covenant partner Jonathan. In essence the two have become one. Amazingly enough this shows that Jonathan is willingly giving up his right to be king!

However, the new covenant found in Jesus Christ is the greatest act in the exchange of robes. We can observe that Jesus exchanged His divine robe for the likeness of a man:

> Who, being in the very nature God, did not consider equality with God something to be grasped, but made himself nothing, taking the very nature of a servant, being made in human likeness. And being found in appearance as a man, he humbled himself and became obedient to death—even death on a cross!
> —PHILIPPIANS 2:6–8, NIV

Jesus fulfilled His destiny as a man by becoming obedient to the point of death on a cross, thus becoming our substitute for sin. This is the new covenant in His blood. Isn't it great that now when God the Father looks at us, He sees us in the righteousness of His Son! I love the words of Martin Luther in "All Praise to Thee, Eternal Lord":

> All praise to Thee, Eternal Lord,
> Clothed in a garb of flesh and blood;
> Choosing a manger for Thy throne,
> While worlds on worlds are Thine alone.[4]

STEP 2: THE EXCHANGE OF BELTS

The military belt was the chief ornament of a soldier and was highly prized in all ancient countries and civilizations. This step represented a partner's willingness to give support and provide strength. Even in European history it was also a rich present from one chieftain to another as it was the symbol of the clan or name of the man and their vow as an ally. The belt was the piece of the wardrobe that held the armor, the swords, and the weapons. By exchanging belts, a person was declaring a responsibility to protect and cover their covenant partner and vice versa—literally saying, "If anybody attacks you, they are attacking me."

Jonathan gave his belt to David as the highest pledge of his esteem and perpetual friendship. (See 1 Samuel 18:4.) This symbolized that if anybody would attack David, they would literally be attacking Jonathan and the entire army he represented. As seen above, David and Jonathan exchanged armor, swords, and bows that were all held together by the belt. Because the belt held a soldier's weapons, it was considered a valuable and desirable part of a soldier's military uniform, and to put on a military belt directly portrayed that men were preparing for battle.

This is not just biblical; it was a sign of the times. From *Troy* when King Priam gives his belt and sword to Hector before battle, to *Robin Hood* when Walter Loxley gives his sword wrapped in its satchel to Robin Longstride, this exemplified tokens of the highest respect and of commitment. However, these were mere tokens of commitment and respect, but God as our covenant partner has committed to fight our battles and be our defender. Deuteronomy 20:4 says, "The LORD your God is the one who goes with you to fight for you against your enemies to give you victory" (NIV).

David had such a keen sense of trust in the Lord. He understood and respected covenant. He knew that if God had anointed him to be the king of Israel, then he would be the king of Israel. David also knew he had a mighty "Covenant Defender" in whom he would place his very life. For example, David had many enemies who pursued him, and David always acknowledges God as his Covenant Defender:

> It is God who arms me with strength and makes my way perfect. He makes my feet like the feet of a deer; he enables me to stand on the heights. He trains my hands for battle; my arms can bend a bow of bronze. You give me your shield and sword of victory, and your right hand sustains me; you stoop down to make me great.
>
> —PSALM 18:32–35, NIV

What is even more amazing is that the new covenant is not conditional to the other person. God is faithful, even when we are unfaithful. With the omnipotent God as our covenant partner, we have access to His inexhaustible strength. Paul explains this exchange in Philippians 4:11–13:

I have learned to be content whatever the circumstances. I know what it is to in need, and I know what it is to have plenty. I have learned the secret of being content in any and every situation, whether well fed or hungry, whether living in plenty or in want. I can do everything through him who gives me strength.

—NIV

However, I think the words to old hymn "Help Us, O Jesus, Thou Mighty Defender" by J. H. Schroder sum it up best:

Help us, O Jesus, Thou mighty Defender,
Help when the forces of evil appear;
Help us to battle and never surrender,
Help us to conquer, and drive away fear;
Satan is cunning, the prince of deceivers,
Bringing disaster to many believers.

Help us, O Jesus, in hours of temptation,
When both our faith and our courage are weak;
Teach us to look to the sign of salvation,
And near Thy cross a new armor to seek;
Then we shall conquer, if Thou wilt befriend us,
Thou wilt prevail and our faith will defend us.

Help us, O Jesus, when death shall spread terror,
And our poor eyes are too feeble to see;
Cleanse us and purge us from sin and from error;
That we may blindly in faith cling to Thee;
Help us, O Jesus, we conquer in dying,
Unto the last on Thy mercy relying.[5]

STEP 3: THE EXCHANGE OF NAMES

The exchange of names is just as one would think it to be. Each covenant partner would take on the meaning and backing of each other's name. But along with the name came the power to use the name. Name exchanges encompass everything that the partner's name represents. Therefore we have access to it. This means that the partners must identify with one another and are expected to think, talk, and act alike.

God exemplifies this in each of His covenantal exchanges, but the primary exchange is when Abram became Abraham and Jehovah God became the God of Abraham (one of the many names of God). Genesis 17 displays that God changed Abram's name to Abraham and his wife Sarai's name to Sarah. The new name, Abraham, means "father of many," but there was a deeper meaning than that in the change. The letter *H*, which was added to Abram's name and to Sarai's name, was from the Lord's own name *Jehovah*. This was a sign that Abraham and Sarah were to be God's children, to obey Him, and as much as humanly possible, to be like Him. Thus, in response to Abraham's faith in this covenant, he was credited for his righteousness.

The closest thing we have in today's society would be the power of attorney. As believers in Jesus Christ, our new covenant is with God our father. The name of Jesus is powerful, and we have access to use the authority of His name: "And whatsoever ye shall ask in my name, that will I do, that the Father may be glorified in the Son" (John 14:13, KJV). The greatest resolve for me comes when Jesus claimed in John 15:16: "You have not chosen me, but I have chosen you, and ordained you, that ye should go and bring forth fruit, and that your fruit should remain: that whatsoever ye shall ask of the Father in my name, he may give it you" (KJV). What power!

STEP 4: THE "CUTTING" OF THE COVENANT

In Hebrew "to make a covenant" literally means "to cut a covenant" (*karat berit*). Biblical covenants were sanctified by cutting animals into two halves. The shedding of blood dramatically ratified and sealed the covenant. (See Genesis 15:9; Jeremiah 34:18–20.) If one attempted to break the covenant, the blood served as a powerful visual lesson that one's own blood would be shed. In brief, it was a solemn oath to be kept on pain of death. It was thus inviolable and irrevocable.

In the Bible there is no covenant that was ever made without the shedding of blood. The "cutting" of the covenant was, in fact, the ceremonial act of the covenant and was demonstrated by cutting an animal in two halves. This style was quite different from the sacrificial cutting of an animal. The animal was laid in two halves with the blood making a pool in the center. The covenant parties would then stand in between the halves with their backs to each other and walk in a figure eight until they would both meet back again in the center. This time, however, they would be facing each other. Eight was and is the unending number—symbolizing the unbroken covenant and eternity.

The covenant parties were bound to each other for eternity, and therefore, a covenant was not taken lightly. The "cutting" of the covenant and walking in between the dead halves of the animal represented the dying of oneself. Additionally, the act of the cutting and the blood flowing represented the giving of one's life for the other—the ultimate act of sacrifice. At this time the covenant partners would vow to each other and exchange words: "I choose this day to die to myself and live to bless you, my covenant partner. I will make my decisions and order my life with you in mind from this day forward; seeking always what is best for you ahead of myself."[6] The other covenant partner would then reply in a similar exchange of words. Together, they would look down at the blood right where they stood and say, "May God do this to me and more if aught but death part you and me."

The Old Testament gives us many examples of what happened to those who broke covenant—death! Joshua 7:1–26 tells how Achan and his entire family were put to death because they took forbidden things from Jericho. However, the entire nation of Israel was cleansed because of the blood of Achan. Similarly, 2 Samuel 21 tells of how Saul broke a covenant agreement with the Gibeonites and seven of Saul's descendants were killed as a result. Harsh, maybe, but Hebrews 9:22 reminds us that God's remedy for broken covenant and sin is: "Without the shedding of blood there is no forgiveness" (NIV).

This powerful ceremony was the very act of the covenant that states to the other party: "You are my first priority." When we came into relationship with God through Jesus Christ, we actually entered into a blood covenant with Him: "For this is My blood of the new covenant, which is shed for many for the remission of sins" (Matt. 26:28). In that moment a divine exchange took place. God released the holy blood of Christ to make atonement for our sins: "Whom God set forth as propitiation by His blood, through faith, to demonstrate His righteousness, because in His forbearance God had passed over the sins that were previously committed" (Rom. 3:25). When

Jesus cut covenant with us, we received all of His assets and He took all our liabilities. Praise God that the blood of Christ is sufficient to cleanse us all from our iniquities, inabilities, and inadequacies. What a deal!

STEP 5: MINGLING OF THEIR BLOOD

Following the cutting of the animals, each person involved in the covenant would make a small cut on their wrist and then clasp their hands together so that the blood would intermingle with each other. Blood symbolizes life, and by the mingling of the blood, the two were carrying out the symbolic act that their lives would be intertwined for all eternity.

God's covenants are everlasting. Just as God made promises to Abraham, so too did Abraham have obligations to God:

> This is my covenant, which ye shall keep, between me and you and thy seed after thee; every man child among you shall be circumcised. And ye shall circumcise the flesh of your foreskin; and it shall be a token of the covenant betwixt me and you.... My covenant shall be in your flesh for an everlasting covenant. And the uncircumcised man child whose flesh of his foreskin is not circumcised, that soul shall be cut off from his people; he hath broken my covenant.
>
> —GENESIS 17:10–14, KJV

STEP 6: MAKE A SCAR

The cut on the back of the right wrist was a deep cut, enough so as to form a scar. This scar would then serve as a permanent reminder of the covenant between the two parties, which became a visible reminder of the terms and rights as a covenant partner. Additionally, the scar became a visible sign to whom the person was connected. At Calvary Jesus endured the scars of the nails through His wrists as a symbol of the covenant He made for you and me through the New Testament.

There is a story of an African missionary by the name of Dr. David Livingstone who traveled and ministered throughout the rural and remote parts of the African jungle. Many of the rural tribes had never encountered or previously seen a white man, which added an additional intrigue as well as a threat to his life. The tribal leaders of the African jungle understood the meaning and depth of covenants and practiced them very closely. Dr. Livingstone cut covenants with more than fifty different tribal leaders. When he would enter a new tribe, he would hold up his wrist as a sign of his covenants. The tribes immediately understood that if they harmed this man, they would be hunted and killed by the other tribes he was in covenant with.[7]

STEP 7: OATH

While still standing in the midst of the blood, the covenant partners would verbally communicate and pledge full release and access to each other's property, money, assets, and so forth. Not only would this exchange entitle them to each other's benefits, but it also held them responsible for each other's liabilities as well.

The Hebrew's original oath with God is known as the *Shema*, which literally means "hear." The *Shema* is from the

Moses text that simply stated: "Hear, O Israel, the LORD our God, the LORD is one" (Mark 12:29). This was not a prayer but a confession of faith or a creed. During the time of Christ, Jesus taught that the greatest commandment was indeed the Shema, but He further explained that we "shall love the LORD your God with all your heart, with all your soul, with all your mind, and with all your strength" (Mark 12:30).

STEP 8: SHARE A MEMORIAL MEAL

Many people today claim the covenant meal is Communion, but it has much deeper roots than today's simple wafer and grape juice that we regularly participate in. Following the above steps, the covenant partners would wash their feet and share a ceremonial meal—different cultures had different types of meals, but the symbolism was the same. Most often the meal involved the breaking of bread and the drinking of wine. Once again the symbolism is rich in that the breaking of bread was equivalent to the cutting of the flesh for one another. However, today we have an obligation to our commemoration during the Lord's Supper or Communion. We have the privilege of receiving a covenant reminder of God's exchange with us.

STEP 9: PLANTING OF A TREE

The last step of the covenant was the planting of a small tree in the spot where the covenant was cut or made. A tree in all cultures represents life. This act of planting marked the covenant as it would grow and bear fruit as it matured due to its deep roots and a firm foundation. For us as believers, we see the new covenant no differently. Following the

Communion meal with His disciples, Jesus went and hung on a tree for all who would merely believe in Him—the ultimate representation of covenant.

Interestingly enough, the term *friend* in the Bible was not used flippantly. *Friend* was used only after a covenant had been made with that person. *Friend* was a serious word that carried the responsibility of covenant. After God made a covenant with Abraham, He called him a "friend of God" (James 2:23). It wasn't until the end of the Last Supper right before the crucifixion that Jesus called His disciples friends: "I no longer call you servants, because a servant does not know his master's business. Instead, I have called you friends, for everything that I learned from my Father I have made known to you" (John 15:15, NIV).

As a covenant partner, now a "friend of God," you are able to exchange all of your mess for all of God's promises and benefits. Read the following scriptures in light of the covenant God has made with his children:

> Most assuredly, I say to you, he who believes in Me, the works that I do he will do also; and greater works than these he will do, because I go to My Father. And whatever you ask in My name, that I will do, that the Father may be glorified in the Son. If you ask anything in My name, I will do it. If you love Me, keep My commandments. And I will pray the Father, and He will give you another Helper, that He may abide with you forever.
>
> —JOHN 14:12–16

You did not choose Me, but I chose you and appointed you that you should go and bear fruit, and that your fruit should remain, that whatever you ask the Father in My name He may give you.

—John 15:16

These things I have spoken to you, that in Me you may have peace. In the world you will have tribulation; but be of good cheer, I have overcome the world.

—John 16:33

And for their sakes I sanctify Myself, that they also may be sanctified by the truth.

—John 17:19

Just as the covenants of old were everlasting, so too is our personal covenant with Jesus Christ. It is a covenant meant to bring us into our eternal destiny. This covenant provides tremendous promises that do give us a hope for our eternal future. But what about this life?

Not only does God have a plan for each of His children to fulfill in this lifetime, but also He longs to give us a future and a hope Therefore He is longing to make a covenant with each of us in order to facilitate that destiny. We must discover God's covenant design for our personal lives. In order to accomplish this, we have to listen, search for Him with all of our hearts, and obey His commandments. You will find Him! In truly understanding this, you must also understand...it's really never over!

For I know the thoughts that I think toward you, says the Lord, thoughts of peace and not of evil, to give you a future and a hope. Then you will call upon Me and go and pray to Me, and I will listen to you. And you will seek Me and find Me, when you search for Me with all your heart.

—JEREMIAH 29:11–13

7

THE PILLARS OF HOPE

*"My hope is built on nothing less than
Jesus' blood and righteousness."*[1]

WHEN THE WORLD says, "Give up," hope whispers, "Try it one more time." Hope has to be one of the pillars on the foundations on which you build your life. Hope is a decision you must make not just today, but every time fear and doubt want to enter your mind or convince you that your situation is over. Regardless of what the conditions look like in the natural, you must *hope*. Hope can heal the hurt.

There is a hope crisis in the world today. People are desperate for hope. And you must, beyond all else, hope.

You may be thinking, "That's all well and good. What a nice idea, Ricardo, to hope. But what does that mean, exactly?"

Today's definition of hope communicates the idea of a wishy-washy lofty dream of some far-off desire that may or may not come true. The standard dictionary definitions define hope as "to *feel* that something desired *may* happen."[2] I'm not sure what comes to your mind when you consider this meaning, but to me *feel* and *may* are two words that hardly exude peace and confidence. On the other hand, biblical hope, the only true hope, is defined as a "strong and confident expectation."[3] *Strong. Confident.* Not merely a feeling that something *may* happen but a confident expectation that it will happen.

There are a few different words used in the Hebrew to define hope. The word *yachal* found in Psalm 33:22 is translated "trust": "Let Your mercy, O Lord, be upon us, just as we hope in You." Other Hebrew translations in the Old Testament are derived from the word *towcheleth*, which is translated "expectation." We are to confidently trust and expect that what God says in His Word is true and *will* come to pass. Not hopefully. Not maybe. They *will* come to pass in God's timing.

To be this confident in God's Word and thus expectant that His will and His Word will come to pass, we have to first be sure of the character of God. A survey of Scripture provides a multitude of verses that testify to God's faithfulness and His constancy. The Bible declares repeatedly that God is trustworthy and is "not a man, that He should lie" (Num. 23:19). That is the very foundation of our hope, that God is who He says He is and that He will do what He says He will do.

Biblical hope will birth joy and peace because you are confident that your life rests in the strong hand of God your Father. Romans 15:13 says:

May the God of your hope so fill you with all joy
and peace in believing [through the experience of your
faith] that by the power of the Holy Spirit you may
abound and be overflowing (bubbling over) with hope.

—AMP

Many years ago I was ministering at a conference in San
Diego with a well-known pastor. During one of the main evening sessions he preached a message called the "Rope of Hope."
Little did I know when I first heard him share this message
that it would minister to my family and me several years later
when Josiah's injury occurred. In his sermon the pastor spoke
about the story in the first four chapters of the Book of Joshua.
The story unfolds following the days after Moses's death and
the nation of Israel crossing the Jordan River to take possession of the Promised Land.

In Joshua chapter 2 we are introduced to Rahab, who lived
in the city of Jericho and was known by her trade as a prostitute. Moses's successor, Joshua, sent two spies into Jericho
to gather information about the city's defenses and its army.
When the spies entered into the city, they sought shelter in
the home of the prostitute Rahab. Though it's not outlined in
the Bible, one of the reasons I believe the spies were inclined
to stay at Rahab's house was because Rahab had a hope for a
better life, and her hope put a demand on the anointing. Your
hope will put a demand on the anointing. When the king of
Jericho learned that two spies from Israel were hiding within
the city walls and came to Rahab demanding access to them,
she lied to protect the spies, saying they had already fled the
city, sending their pursuers on a wild goose chase. Then listen
to what Rahab told the spies in Joshua 2:9–13:

I know that the LORD has given you the land, and that the fear of you has fallen upon us, and that all the inhabitants of the land melt away before you. For we have heard how the LORD dried up the water of the Red Sea before you when you came out of Egypt, and what you did to the two kings of the Amorites that were beyond the Jordan, to Sihon and Og, whom you devoted to destruction. And as soon as we heard it, our hearts melted, and there was no spirit left in any man because of you, for the LORD your God, he is God in the heavens above and on the earth beneath. Now then, please swear to me by the LORD that, as I have dealt kindly with you, you also will deal kindly with my father's house, and give me a sure sign that you will save alive my father and mother, my brothers and sisters, and all who belong to them, and deliver our lives from death.

—ESV

This woman of pagan upbringing, a prostitute by occupation, recognized and believed in her heart that the Lord, the God of Israel, is God of heaven and on earth (v. 11). I believe Rahab was sensitive to the presence of God in the two spies and had a hope that God had more for her than her current situation. Obviously it was God ordained, but it is interesting to me that the only persons who were saved when the Israelites laid siege to the city of Jericho were Rahab and her family. It doesn't matter who you are or where you've come from; your hope or faith in God can change not only your life but also the life of the generations that follow you. Going back to verses 12 and 13 we can see how she petitions the two men of God to rescue her and her family from the coming devastation of her city.

> Now then, please swear to me by the LORD that, as I have dealt kindly with you, you also will deal kindly with my father's house, and give me a sure sign that you will save alive my father and mother, my brothers and sisters, and all who belong to them, and deliver our lives from death.
>
> —ESV

The two spies were moved by Rahab's faith to offer her protection, and in that bold and courageous act she saved herself and her family from destruction and certain death. The Bible says in Joshua 2:17–19:

> The men told her, "In order to keep this oath you made us swear, here is what you must do: Hang this red rope out the window through which you let us down and gather your entire family with you in your house—father, mother, brothers, sisters. Anyone who goes out the doors of your house into the street and is killed, it's his own fault—we aren't responsible. But for everyone within the house we take full responsibility.
>
> —THE MESSAGE

So Rahab hung the "rope of hope" from her window as a sign of the promise of protection from the men of Israel, and Rahab was provided salvation from the destruction that overtook Jericho. Hope can change the course of your life. Hope can set you in a different direction!

Hope to Stay Afloat

Dr. Jerome Groopman states in his book *The Anatomy of Hope:*

> Clear-eyed, hope gives us the courage to confront our circumstances and the capacity to surmount them. For all my patients, hope, true hope, has proved as important as any medication I might prescribe or any procedure I might perform.[4]

Hope is such a powerful emotion that it has even been shown to improve the condition of terminally ill patients in the hospital and replace treatments such as chemotherapy. The Cancer Wellness Center makes it clear that "we all live through hope. What we hope for changes as we travel through life, but hope remains a constant necessity for life. Hope is at the very heart of healing."[5] The connection between hope and the human spirit is studied by medical science as a means of healing and alternative medicine.

There is a medical story of a patient known as Mrs. Brown. Mrs. Brown was a sixty-nine-year-old widow with no known family who was diagnosed with metastatic breast cancer. After enduring several chemotherapy and radiotherapy sessions, the disease continued to worsen, and the symptoms raided her body. Mrs. Brown was emaciated, depressed, and hopeless. Due to her worsening condition, Mrs. Brown's oncologist suggested a break from therapy to allow her body to recovery nutritionally from the invasive treatments.

During the interim Mrs. Brown was checked into a hospice program, where her entrance interview revealed to the nursing staff that she had an estranged daughter with whom she hadn't spoken to or seen in more thirty years. Through diligent efforts the social workers arranged for a meeting between Mrs. Brown and her daughter. The *hope* of reuniting with her daughter began to improve Mrs. Brown's spirits. Her focus and efforts were pointed toward a goal, an expectation, a newfound hope. Mrs. Brown chose to forgo further chemotherapy and continued to see improved health with the potential renewal of her relationship with her daughter.[6]

Though, as Christians, our hope is based on more than an emotion, the medical connection, I believe, was intentional in our design by God. The emotion of hope releases endorphins in the brain and lifts the human spirit from despair and depression. James Averill, a social constructivist, believes hope is a learned emotion. Hope is something you must teach yourself and train your brain to think using patterns and positions of hope. Averill's research indicates that the presence of hope has five distinctive features:

1. Hope can be difficult to control.

2. Hope affects the way you think or perceive events.

3. Hope affects the way you behave.

4. Hope motivates behavior, increases persistence, and enables one to go on (even in the face of adversity).

5. Hope is a common universal experience.[7]

In the event of complete despair, you must hope in order to stay afloat of life's circumstance. Hopelessness removes the veil of what Jesus did. Your hope is your life preserver in the ocean of "it's not over." Sometimes life can look like an ocean with no shore in sight, but hope is the raft that will get you to shore. Stay afloat on the boat of hope.

FIRST THINGS FIRST

As a traveling minister, I am sometimes in three to four states a week jetting back and forth between different time zones. Before long my body and my muscles begin to ache with the tension and stress of maintaining such a harried pace for extended periods of time. In an attempt to relieve this unwanted discomfort in my physical body, I started seeing a chiropractor. One of the first things she wanted to check was to see if my body was out of alignment. When the doctor completed her evaluation, she said, "Ricardo, you're a wreck! You are so out of alignment. When you are out of alignment, you are prone to more injuries."

That's just like life. When matters such as relationships, values, or priorities are out of alignment, your life is increasingly more prone to injuries. We're not talking sore muscles and a bad back here; these are wounds to the heart. When first things aren't first and your life's priorities become unclear, there is a danger that your attention and energy will be spent pursuing inconsequential goals. This could be a parent and spouse devoting every ounce of their time and energy to advance a career while on the other hand neglecting to invest any time at all in their family at home. The career-driven parent might not even be aware of the potential emotional or psychological injuries, feelings of rejection or abandonment, for example, suffered by the spouse and children. This is not to say that having a successful career in and of itself indicates improper priorities; in fact, I believe it is very rewarding and honorable to provide for your family by the sweat of your brow from an honest day's work. The difference is illustrated by the appropriate amount of value and attention given to the care and well-being of the family in relation to the career. Nor am I implying that advancing in your career and having a happy home are exclusive of each other. But we must pay careful attention to keep our values and priorities in alignment, holding tightly to our children, spouse, parents, friends, honor, integrity, godly character, and the like, while holding loosely to those things that if not tempered with wisdom can throw our lives out of balance.

When you're spiritually out of alignment, it's easier to get discouraged, it's easier to get upset, and it's easier to get angry. It's easier to not give as much because you're exhausted and out of alignment.

In 2 Chronicles chapter 20 we read that a vast army was marching toward Jerusalem preparing to attack King Jehoshaphat and his people. King Jehoshaphat kept his priorities in order. With calamity and destruction bearing down on him, he turned his attention to God. The Bible does not say the king was unaffected upon hearing news of this approaching army. In fact, different translations say he was alarmed, shaken, and that he feared (v. 3). But what he did next demonstrated that he was in alignment spiritually, for he immediately set himself to seek the Lord.

How about that? Is our first reaction to seek the Lord when we hear that something bad has happened? Or do we instead follow the force of natural inertia and allow panic and fear to chart our course of action? King Jehoshaphat knew the God he trusted, and he immediately aligned himself to be in a position to hear God's counsel. He declared a fast for the entire nation of Judah, stood in the assembly of the people in the house of the Lord, and one by one recited the multitude of occasions where God had rescued His people from harm. In doing so he encouraged himself and his people by remembering God's faithfulness through the generations.

In verse 12 Jehoshaphat ended this time of worship declaring to God, "We do not know what to do, but our eyes are upon you" (NIV). When God responded, it was to remind the king and all the people of Judah not to be afraid, "for the battle is not yours, but God's" (v. 15). The next morning, as King Jehoshaphat went out to see the deliverance of the Lord, he sent out singers before the armies to sing songs of praise and to worship the Lord. He knew that when you keep your praise in front of everything you do, your hope and mind-set stay aligned with the things of God.

ARMOR OF HOPE

Hope can actually function as armor of protection for yourself and your family. In chapter 6 of Paul's letter to the Ephesians, Paul writes about taking up the shield of faith as one of the six pieces of the armor of God, referring to hope as faith. When Paul uses to the word *shield*, it was a very different *shield* than you and I are familiar with today. You have probably seen any number of movies or superhero cartoons that depict a warrior or soldier defending himself with a shield the shape of a simple round disk, just about the size of a large pizza, similar to the shield carried by Captain America. In ancient Rome the shields most commonly used were circular in shape. But the shield in biblical times, when Paul would have addressed the Ephesians, was quite another model.

Referred to as a *scutum*, the Latin word for "shield," a term later adopted by the Byzantine military, this model of shield was rectangular in shape and utilized very effectively throughout history by many a Roman legionnaire. The *scutum* was generally about three and a half feet tall and sometimes as much as three feet wide with curved edges, sizable enough to cover a considerable portion of the soldier's body but light enough to be held with one arm. These shields could be joined together side by side to create a moveable wall and raised overhead to protect from arrows, rocks, and other falling debris. The design was intentional, created in such a way that the soldier would not feel the weight of the oncoming attack, the curved edges deflecting the pressure of a blow away from the person carrying the *scutum* or shield.

That is exactly what hope is designed to do. The pressure of life and the weight of your circumstances are not supposed to be carried by you. When you hold onto hope and lift the shield of faith, any attacks from the enemy should be deflected without you bearing the weight of the burden. Hope deflects the weight of your problem!

There is a story in 2 Kings that I would love to show you. To preface this story, let me explain that the Israelites had been suffering a severe famine prior to when we will join the scene. The famine was so severe, in fact, that some people had resorted to cannibalism because there seemed to be no other alternative means of survival. When you lose hope, you resort to doing things and acting in ways you would never have thought possible. Hopelessness breeds desperation. The

Israelites were desperate, and there seemed to be no hope in site. No answers. No solutions. What food there was to be found was being sold at such an astronomical price that the people of Israel were unable to afford anything. Entire villages were starving, and the people were terrified at the uncertainty of what was going to happen to them and their families. It sounds very similar to the present-day economy in certain countries around the world.

At the beginning of 2 Kings chapter 7, Elisha prophesied that the famine would come to an end within twenty-four hours, but because of the desperate and severe state of the economy, nobody could believe that it was possible. In the natural a dramatic reversal of conditions this severe seemed completely and utterly impossible. In the midst of the famine there were four lepers, the Bible says, who were forced to live outside the city gate, condemned to isolation by their disease. Now let me explain; in that day and age leprosy was pretty much the curse of death. Today it would be similar to having a disease like AIDS, especially a few decades ago when very little information was known about the AIDS virus. Like the AIDS virus, leprosy was an incurable disease that, at the time of our story, completely removed anyone who had contracted the disease from all social and religious gatherings. While leprosy itself was not a fatal disease, from the moment an individual was stricken with leprosy, they were promptly ostracized and sentenced to live a life shared only by others in the same lamentable situation. If there was any physical condition that seemed hopeless, leprosy was it. Living a life with leprosy was essentially a living death. I take the time to expound on leprosy because there couldn't have been any situation that seemed so impossible or a condition that was quite so hopeless as leprosy. But watch how God works and intervenes in the lives of the four lepers in this story.

Left to themselves outside the city gates, these four pitiable souls had plenty of time to sit and consider the state of their woes. On the very same day Elisha prophesied that the famine was about to end, there the four sat discussing the volume and frequency of the rumblings in their respective stomachs, trying to remember the last time they had enjoyed a hot meal. After they had each had opportunity to share their peace, they came to a unanimous decision. Together the four lepers had concluded that their condition in life was pretty much hopeless; death seemed to be waiting for them no matter which way they turned. Since they were starving from the famine anyway, they decided to visit the adjoining Aramean army and see if the army would have compassion on them and offer them food and water. The four lepers figured that even if the Arameans refused to show them kindness and killed them, it wouldn't matter because they were doomed to die anyway.

So it was then that as the sun set and the warm glow of twilight faded into the gray dusk of evening, the four lepers set out to visit the Aramean camp in hopes of receiving benevolence. However, upon entering the camp, the lepers found nothing but the Aramean army's horses, clothing, food, and all of their personal belongings left for the lepers to collect as their spoils. The lepers had hit the lottery! The Bible says the Lord caused the Aramean army to hear the sound of chariots and horses. The Arameans thought they were under attack and fled, leaving everything that had been in their possession to be collected by the Israelites.

Here's what is so incredible. God chose to bring restoration to the Israelites through something they considered, in the natural, hopeless and useless. God will use those things around you that appear to be dead to resurrect new answers and direction in your life. The lepers had hoped for a better solution and acted on their hope. When you act on the hope inside you, God will take what you thought was useless and turn around the areas of famine in your life.

The lepers left their current situation with nothing more than hope, and their hope transformed their lives. The Bible says the Arameans heard the sound of chariots and horses and fled because they thought they were under attack. Hope will make your enemies think you are stronger than you really are! Hope is an armor that can cover and protect in the midst of life's battles. Use the armor of hope against your enemy.

POSITION OF HOPE

In the midst of our "it's not over" moment—the chaos and confusion of Josiah being airlifted to the children's hospital in downtown Atlanta, my trying to find the first available flight back from Florida to get to the hospital as quickly as possible, Jennette rushing to the emergency room to be with Josiah, and still waiting for the doctors to give us some sort of idea that Josiah was going to be OK—we had nothing but our hope to stand on. We sent text messages to friends, family, and pastors all around the country asking them to pray for our son, but we had to have the hope that God was in control. Hope was what we leaned on and pushed against for support. Hope was the position from which we *had* to stand. Our son's life was hanging in the balance. We had no choice but to hope.

Then when Jennette received that out-of-the-blue, breakthrough call from a neurologist friend in California, we knew that hope had brought a turnaround in our situation. His words, "Mrs. Sanchez, I want you to know, I spoke with the emergency room. Your son is going to be OK. Josiah will walk again," meant so much to us. And in that moment we were able to see the truth of Romans 5:5: "Now hope does not disappoint, because the love of God has been poured out in our hearts by the Holy Spirit who was given to us."

There is a position of hope that not only puts you in a position to see the miracle but also for the miracle to see you! In Luke 19 the Bible talks about the tax collector Zacchaeus who desperately wanted to see Jesus:

> Then Jesus entered and walked through Jericho. There was a man there, his name Zacchaeus, the head tax man and quite rich. He wanted to desperately to see Jesus, but the crowd was in his way—he was a short man and couldn't see over the crowd. So he ran on ahead and climbed up in a sycamore tree so he could see Jesus when he came by.
> —Luke 19:1–4, The Message

There are times and seasons in life when you won't be able to see Jesus because of the crowd. Whatever "the crowd" represents in your life—whether it's trials, poor choices, the pressure of life—it will block your view of Jesus. The Bible says that Zacchaeus was a short man and couldn't see over the crowd. He was not capable of seeing over his crowd because he was in the wrong position. So Zacchaeus "ran on ahead and climbed up in a sycamore tree so he could see Jesus when he came by." In the natural Zacchaeus was limited by his height, but he positioned himself to see his answer.

Zacchaeus changed his position. I've always been told that Zacchaeus climbed the tree so he could see Jesus, but I also believed he climbed the tree so Jesus could see him. When you choose to change your position to one of hope, you put yourself in a position not only for you to see Jesus but also for Jesus to see you! The position of hope elevates you above your circumstances. It changes your view.

Once Zacchaeus chose to climb the tree, the crowd that was once in his way wasn't even an issue any more. The position of hope puts you above the ordinary. It lifts you above those things that press against you and want to push you away from Jesus. Another thing: because Zacchaeus changed his position, Jesus had dinner at Zacchaeus's house that night. By Zacchaeus changing his position, he opened the door for his miracle to walk in and have dinner with him! The position of hope will elevate you above the ordinary and open the door for a miracle to walk in!

We ended up staying in the hospital with Josiah a little over two weeks, during which time we had a steady stream of friends and family stop in to celebrate our miracle with us. The love and support we felt from each person who took the time to call, write, send flowers, and pray with us over a coffee in the first-floor family lounge of the hospital are treasured memories we will always carry with us. Over the course of those weeks in the hospital our friends and family came alongside us holding out hope for us when we were feeling the weight of physical exhaustion and the stress and strain as a result of the situation. We were able to draw strength from

our friends and standing shoulder to shoulder with them—
like the soldiers with their shields linked together—and we
continue to expect His will and His word to come to pass in
our lives.

However, of all the people who came and poured out their
love upon our family, one visit in particular was very significant. Right after the accident a friend of ours made a surprise
visit one morning. Our friend told Jennette and me that both
she and her daughter had identical dreams about Josiah on the
same night. In their dreams they saw that when Josiah hit the
bottom of the pool there was an angel there who picked Josiah
up and said, "It's not over!" Sometimes it may feel as if you
are all alone and that everyone, including God, has deserted
you, but you may never know the times an unforeseen angel
has picked you up and covered you only by the grace of God.

8

DON'T WAIT TO CELEBRATE

"Bless the Lord, O my soul, and all that is within me, Bless His holy name."[1]

I F YOU HAVE a family, I'm sure you're aware how important celebrations are. If your kids are like mine, they are planning their next birthday party the day after they celebrated their current birthday party or they start making their Christmas lists in January. The truth of the matter is people love to be celebrated. There is something special about feeling special. No matter how old you get, you still like to be celebrated. You still like to know that you are loved and that those people around you hold you in high esteem. Celebrations are about remembering someone special or a special event in life.

Former and Latter

Though it's an example in its simplest form, did you know God loves to celebrate? God is constantly throwing a party and enjoying the beauty of His creation. In Leviticus God instructed the Israelites to celebrate seven feasts throughout the year. Absolutely. There are seven feasts in the Bible that the law required the Israelites to celebrate. Here's what is so interesting. The early feasts celebrated and commemorated the things that Christ had already done, and the latter feasts or festivals celebrated the events that Christ was still going to do. Let me reiterate. The first four feasts celebrated victories the Israelites had *already* received and experienced, and the remaining three feasts celebrated victories the Israelites hadn't experienced yet but knew they were promises made by God. The feasts celebrated what God *did* and the feasts celebrated what God *will do.* The celebrations were about the past and the future. The celebrations were about the "former" and the "latter" rain. Though the feasts of the Lord provide a detailed and foreshadowed view of the return of our Messiah, I also believe the feasts of the Lord provide a template of how we are to celebrate.

We honor and celebrate the things that have already happened: a birthday, an anniversary, and certain benchmarks. But as children of God we must also celebrate the things He is going to do. You must be intentional and celebrate the things God has done in your life, and you must celebrate the things God is going to do in your life. You have to celebrate the victories that have passed and the victories that are still yet to come.

When Jennette and I had crossed the hurdle of first

learning that Josiah was going to live and walk, we then had to encounter the fact that there was a lengthy surgery with lifelong results—things such as limited mobility and certain activities that Josiah will never be able to participate in. However, we didn't focus on the things Josiah was not going to be able to do. We celebrated the things we knew he would be able to do. We would say things such as, "Praise God, Josiah, you are going to be a walking, talking, breathing miracle! God is going to use you to build faith in other people to believe for their own healing." Even when Jennette and I would be praying alone together, we would pray, "Thank You, God, that Josiah will have full motion of his neck, that his limitations will be minimal, and his breathing stabilized." We celebrated and believed for those things we knew God could do and those things God already had done. If you saw Josiah today, other that the physical scars on his neck, you would have no idea he endured and experienced what he had.

As a worship leader I love the verse in Psalm 22:3 that says that God "inhabitest the praises of Israel" (KJV). I would like to make something clear; praise has nothing to do with music. You can praise with or without music. You can celebrate with or without a choir behind you. You can praise loudly or quietly. You can praise with your eyes closed or open. Celebration, praise, and worship are attitudes of the heart and have nothing to do with music.

Now I am not suggesting that you praise God for the mess you are in. I'm telling you that you should praise God because He is on the throne. When you praise and lift high the name of the Lord above the mess that you are in, His presence is sure to visit you *in* your mess. In essence, what I'm saying is don't praise Him because of the mess; praise Him while you're in the mess. There's a praise that celebrates what He's already done, and there's a praise that celebrates what He's about to do! Celebrate the former and the latter.

Waiting to celebrate the victory until you see it with your eyes is like making the mistake that joy and laughter are the same thing. Let me explain. The word *joy* and its different variations are mentioned more than two hundred times in the Bible. As Christians we are supposed to be joyful. Did you know the word *laughter* is mentioned only forty-two times, and of those times it is mentioned, it is often used as a mockery of evil? Joy and laughter are not the same thing. You can laugh and not have joy. Laughing refers to something that is for the moment, but joy is an attitude of the heart and is eternal.

Fun and joy are two different things. You might not be having fun when your bills are piled high with no idea how you will be able to pay them, or when the house is chaotic and your marriage isn't where you'd like it to be, but you can still have joy. Fun is predicated on your external environment, and joy is predicated on your internal environment. Joy is not associated with a life that is free from trials, nor is joy equated with comfort or pure bliss. Joy is not an emotion. It is a choice. Celebrating those things you have not yet seen is a choice. It is a choice you must make today. It is a choice you must make tomorrow. It is a choice you must make if you are walking through a circumstance that looks like there is no hope. You must have joy and continue to believe and profess, "It's not over." Psalm 16:11 tells us exactly where joy can be found:

You will show me the path of life; in Your presence is fullness of joy; at Your right hand are pleasures forevermore.

The only place to find joy is in His presence. True joy, true contentment, true peace is only found in the presence of the Lord. Your source of joy is not your husband, not your wife, not children, not your job; nor is it your pastor or your church. Your source of joy is God and God alone.

SHOUT OUT

When I was waiting at the airport to get back to my son, fear, doubt, and destruction were shouting loud at me. There are times in life when you need to shout louder than what's shouting at you. When I was at the airport not knowing how my story would end, I was shouting out with a fearless abandonment for my son's healing. I believe that certain circumstances in life will not break without the people of God issuing a shout!

There have been some interesting discoveries about the ability of invisible sound waves. I was reading an article that said sound waves, which are not seen by the eye, actually have the ability to break solids, which are seen by the eye.[2] Sound waves can cause a glass, for example, to shatter. I'm sure you've seen the demonstration on television with an amazing high-pitched opera singer hitting the right note and a glass crumbling. In order for the glass to break, the sound wave and the object must be at the *same frequency*.

There are situations in your life that require a unique frequency. I recognize that you can't walk around life screaming, but I am saying that there is a heavenly frequency that you tap into when you change your frequency into a celebration of worship.

In Joshua 6 Joshua led the Israelites around the city of Jericho. In Joshua 6:1 the Bible says, "Now Jericho was securely shut up because of the children of Israel…" Jericho was the promise they were seeking. Jericho was where they were headed, but the Bible says, It was "securely shut up." Their promise was locked up.

Have you ever felt as if your promise is locked up? You know what God has said you are to inherit, but it is unattainable, somehow out of your reach. There seems to be a wall between you and your promise. God had promised Jericho to the Israelites, but the road from the promise to the manifestation was not what they expected. Remember the Israelites wandered in the desert for forty years and really had to learn to trust God and trust His provision. The Israelites had to wander the desert in order to get the "desert mentality" out of their hearts. A whole generation had to pass away, along with some bad attitudes and wrong patterns of thinking.

The Israelites were instructed to march around Jericho for six days. On the seventh day they were instructed to march around the walls seven times and then blow their trumpets. It wasn't the Israelites complaining that brought the walls down. It wasn't their begging or their crying. The walls of Jericho came down when they lifted their shout in unison to God. The Israelite's promise was released when they lifted their shout. Joshua 6:5 says:

It shall come to pass, when they make a long blast with the ram's horn, and when you hear the sound of the trumpet, that all the people shall shout with a great shout; then the wall of the city will fall down flat.

Sometimes the only thing between you and your promise is a shout. Sometimes those things locked behind walls are being held back and are waiting for you to lift your voice and celebrate with a shout! Your situation, your promise, your "it's not over" moment needs a shout of worship to God in acknowledgement for what He's done and for what He's about to do.

Celebrate in Your Own Way

You may be saying to yourself, "That shouting 'stuff' just isn't for me. It's just not my personality. I didn't grow up that way." Please understand; I am not here to tell you how you need to worship. I recognize and understand every person is different, and each person has a different way of expressing himself. To each his own. Not a problem. But why is it that when you go to the football game, you stand on your feet acting like a maniac for your team, not only shouting, but shouting with your hands in the air? Listen, I believe God should receive your highest and best celebrations. If you're a quiet "shouter," then great. But be consistent, and don't make justifications about your worship. I've generally found those people who aren't comfortable acknowledging God in worship are lacking intimacy in some way in their relationship with Him. Whether it's shouting, lifting your hands, singing quietly, or quietly observing, always pursue a more intimate relationship with God.

On that same note I'd like to take a brief minute and direct these next few sentences to the men reading this book. I've found that, in general, it's the men who have a difficult time outwardly expressing their worship to God. Somehow society has said it's not masculine, cool, or acceptable for men to worship God.

Men, your family needs you to be the leader of your home in all areas, but first and foremost in the area of worship. Your children are watching how you interact with God, and they will emulate the relationship they see. You must set a godly example of a praying, worshiping father who is first submitted to His heavenly Father. Leave your children a monetary inheritance, but also leave them a spiritual inheritance and lead them in the things of God.

Generally it is the people who have been set free from deep bondage, addictions, or very dark sins who are able to have the most expressive and outward worship. The way worship is expressed is, of course, individual and unique to every person. Although we may not understand how or why people worship they way they do, we must never criticize or judge the humility, honor, and utter awe that person has in the presence of God. As fathers, and even as children of God, you should want your children and those around you to be affected and infected by your contagious worship. You should want them to see, from your worship, the impact God has had on your life, not just when the music is playing, but also during your daily life.

Several years ago Jennette and I had the opportunity to

attend a concert for a well-known Christian artist. We were in the Glendale arena in Arizona with about twenty thousand other people and were sitting about seven rows in front of the stage. Seated a few rows in front of us was a lady who was obviously enjoying the concert and was very visibly expressing her worship by dancing and freely moving to the music. A few seats behind this lady were two other couples who were well dressed and perhaps from upper-class suburbia. The ladies carried exquisite purses and the husbands had on very expensive watches. Both couples, whether they had money or not, were very clearly trying to communicate the message of wealth or were desperately trying to act as people who had their act together.

As the concert went on, Jennette and I began to observe a situation that truly broke my heart. The well-dressed, "flashy" couples began to mock and outwardly make fun of the "free-worshiper." It was so rude and so embarrassing that the spirit of *righteous indignation,* if you know what I mean, rose up in me. I wanted to take the men outside and give them a lesson on the "fist of the spirit"—I mean, "the fruit of the Spirit." Right about that same time my wife nudged me, and I heard the voice of the Lord within my spirit (or maybe it was my wife, sometimes they are the same voice—if you're married, you know what I mean) say, "Ricardo, those people have no idea what I've delivered this lady from and why she can worship so freely! Her worship has come at a great price. You have no idea what she's been set free from or the heaviness she used to carry." Watching this scenario unfold so spoke to my spirit that there is a freedom that comes from being set free. This moment was the inspiration that birthed the song

"I'm Not Ashamed." The lyrics became a prayer in my own life as an attitude of pure worship between Jesus and me. Read a short part of the chorus and worship without regard to what people think:

I'm going to dance for You
Like nobody's watching; nobody's watching
Dance for You, my Lord.
I'm going to sing for You
Like nobody's listening; nobody's listening
Sing for You, my Lord.
I'm not holding anything, anything back
I will worship You with all that I am
I'm not ashamed
To worship the name of Jesus, Jesus.[3]

Just as it was with the lady at the concert, you have no idea when you see people worshiping what they have been delivered from, where they came from, or the heaviness they may have just laid at the feet of Jesus.

In Matthew 26:7 there is a story, similar to the one I mentioned above, about a woman who brought her expensive alabaster box full of perfume and poured it on the head of Jesus. The disciples were indignant and upset that this lady would waste such an expensive asset. When Jesus heard how upset these people were at the lady's expression of worship, Jesus said, "Leave this lady alone. She has just done something wonderfully significant for Me" (vv. 10–11). Like the alabaster box, your time of intimacy with God is valuable. People might not understand why you would "waste" your time on something, but to God your worship is significant.

Personally, I'm passionate in what I do, and I enjoy seeing passion in others. Honestly, it wouldn't excite me very much if when I returned home from a weeklong ministry trip and walked in the door, Jennette was sitting on the couch reading a book and only briefly looked up to give me a quick nod. Thankfully, she doesn't do that. When I come home from being gone, even if it's a day, my boys coming running and shouting, "Daddy's home!" Jennette greets me at the door with a hug, a kiss, and sincere joy that I'm back home. I love that! I believe God is the same way. I believe He loves when we celebrate and honor who He is and what He has done for us. Psalm 33:3 says, "Invent your own new song to him; give him a trumpet fanfare" (THE MESSAGE). I believe God enjoys when we celebrate Him.

THE VOICE OF AUTHORITY

As the youngest of five boys and one girl, there was often chaos in my house growing up. All six of us Sanchez kids were born within seven years, and we were constantly getting into some sort of trouble.

My mother was a saint. We didn't have much, but my parents somehow managed to keep us kids fed and clothed. All five of us boys shared one room, which was no bigger than fifteen feet by fifteen feet. I'm sure you can imagine, bedtime was a nightmare for my mother, especially when we were younger. It wouldn't take long after being sent to sleep, before one of my brothers would be up jumping on the bed, throwing a pillow, and begging for a fight. Despite the number of times my mother would shout, "Go to sleep, boys!" or come into our room to settle us down, we knew we would be given another chance.

But there was something different when my father spoke. There was an immediate authority recognized in my father's voice. It would take only one time hearing, "Hey, quiet down in there!", and all of us kids would be scrambling to get under the covers because we knew he would shortly be coming in with his belt.

As children of God there is an authority that comes with your shout that leaves your enemy scrambling. The Bible says in Romans 8:11, "But if the Spirit of Him who raised Jesus from the dead dwells in you, He who raised Christ from the dead will also give life to your mortal bodies through His Spirit who dwells in you." You have the same authority as God when you come in the name of Jesus against your circumstances. It doesn't matter if you shout, if you speak, or if you whisper—it's not the delivery; it's the name of Jesus that gets the attention of heaven. The Bible says in Philippians 2:10, "At the name of Jesus every knee should bow, of those in heaven, and of those on earth, and of those under the earth, and that every tongue should confess that Jesus Christ is Lord, to the glory of God the Father."

9

DON'T FORGET TO REMEMBER

"All glory and praise to the God of all grace, who hast brought us and sought us and guided our ways. Hallelujah!"[1]

N LIFE THERE are things we forget to remember, and there are things we remember that we need to forget. Why is it that you can remember the anniversary your husband forgot eight years ago, but you forget how God miraculously provided an answer in the midst of a desperate situation? Or why can you remember the person who misused you in a business deal many moons ago, but you don't remember the time God opened a door for a new contract when you were under the gun to meet a quota? You've forgotten that you used to cry out and plead with God to provide you with a godly spouse. Now you only remember that he or she didn't clean the bathroom or take out the trash! Am I making the picture clear?

Why as men can we remember who won the Super Bowl in 1977 or how many home runs Sammy Sosa hit 1998, but we can't remember to pray with our children or tell our wives how beautiful they look? It is easy to forget the important things and remember the unimportant things, but you must remember the important things and forget the unimportant things. You must make a choice to remember the things God has done for you, and you must also make a choice to forget those things or situations in life that have wronged you.

The power of your memory and the interaction with your brain is amazing. In the simplest form scientists have learned that a memory is retrieved by the communication between what is called the synapses and neurons, which send and receive electrical signals and act as the pathways and receptors for information in your brain. Without getting too technical, when you remember something, neurons fire down signals to synapse pathways, which in turn fire signals to other neurons. This particular sequence represents a memory. I found it so interesting to learn that scientists have actually been able to stimulate memory and enable people to "relive" experiences from the past by poking around in their brains with electric probes and starting this interaction between the synapses and neurons.

When you remember things that are unimportant, you have to spend the time and energy focusing on that memory in order to re-create that "pathway" mentioned above in your brain for those thoughts to easily be recalled. Without the pathway those memories are forgotten. The things you've forgotten are not brought up often because that pathway between neurons and synapses in your brain has not been traveled very often. The recall of and focus on memories is what makes them permanent in your brain. What I'm saying is that when you remember things you need to forget, you've spent time focusing on them and recalling them from your brain. You need to spend time focusing on the things that are important. You must build memorials in your life to remember the good things and the God things. Otherwise they are easy to forget.

BUILD A MEMORIAL

If you're like me there are certain days in history that will forever be etched into your heart. September 11, 2001, has been and will be one of those days in my life. I'll never forget getting a phone call to quickly turn on the television. As I sat and watched the first plane fly into tower number one, the horror, hurt, and handicap I felt were surreal and overwhelming. America was forever changed—how we fly, how we interface with the Middle East, our military… Words such as "we'll never forget" began to be included in country songs and television commercials, and the process of erecting a memorial began. Ten years later to the day a memorial was opened to the families of those fallen heroes who lost their lives in the tragedy of 9/11, which was felt by America but experienced around the world. I watched as mothers, sons, fathers, grandparents, daughters, wives, and husbands wept as they walked through and found their loved one's name artistically carved into stone in memory of the life they gave up, some voluntarily and some involuntarily.

Memorials are powerful. Memorials are set up to honor.

Memorials are tangible pieces of history because, as people, we tend to forget. Sure my generation might never forget what happened on 9/11, but my sons, who didn't share that memory, might not remember the importance of that day, and my grandchildren will only read about the events that happened on 9/11 in a history book. Memorials connect generations and remind us of what could easily be forgotten.

Memorials are so important to God that, on multiple occasions, He instructed His people to erect a memorial or to make an altar in memory of what He had done for that generation. In Joshua 4, following the miraculous exodus from Egypt when the Israelites crossed on dry ground, God instructed the Israelites to build a memorial.

In Joshua 4:1–7 read how God instructed the Israelites once they had crossed the river:

> When all the people had crossed the Jordan, the LORD said to Joshua, "Now choose twelve men, one from each tribe. Tell them, 'Take twelve stones from the very place where the priests are standing in the middle of the Jordan. Carry them out and pile them up at the place where you will camp tonight.'"
>
> So Joshua called together the twelve men he had chosen—one from each of the tribes of Israel. He told them, "Go into the middle of the Jordan, in front of the Ark of the LORD your God. Each of you must pick up one stone and carry it out on your shoulder—twelve stones in all, one for each of the twelve tribes of Israel. We will use these stones to build a memorial. In the future your children will ask you, 'What do these stones mean?' Then you can tell them, 'They

remind us that the Jordan River stopped flowing when the Ark of the LORD's Covenant went across.' These stones will stand as a memorial among the people of Israel forever."

—NLT

God told the Israelites, one person from each tribe, to go and grab a stone from the middle of the Jordan River and bring it with them to the other side. In essence God said, "Go and grab a memory from when you were *right in the middle* of your mess, when you weren't sure how it was all going to work out and there seemed to be no solution. Take a stone right from the middle of the river. Take one of those stones, and each of you bring it here and build a memorial, so that when the future generations see this pile of twelve stones and they ask why they are there, you'll be able to say, 'You see, there was a time when we had no idea how we were going to cross the river, and we thought it was over, but God made a way when there seemed to be no way!'" Your children need to know the things God has done for you. Your future generations need to know that it took some faith and it took some fighting, but God saw you through, and your memorials are a reminder to His faithfulness and provision.

When we got home from the hospital, Josiah was inundated with posters and cards and pictures hung all around the house from neighbors and family who flew into town to help. We've since created a memorial book for Josiah with pictures of him in the hospital, pictures of him wearing his neck brace, pictures of the posters saying "Miracle Boy," and pictures of Josiah post-healing and playing basketball in the gym with his trainer. We put together a memorial for Josiah to always look back and remember what God brought him through and how significant his injures could have been if it wasn't for the hand of God on his life. Josiah will always have an altar and a tangible point of contact to show his children and his children's children how God's faithfulness covered him. A memorial can be a point of contact for your faith and a reminder that if God brought you through once, He can bring you through again!

COMMUNION REUNION

Remembering what God has done and setting up memorials for you and your family is a valuable place to stand when life *doesn't* go as planned or, for that matter, when life *does* go as planned. When you look back and remember God's faithfulness in your life, your faith is spurred to know that God is going to continue to be faithful to you in the future. Communion is the most important memorials for the Christian faith.

If you remember, the original Communion or Last Supper was celebrated with Jesus and His disciples right before Jesus went to the cross to be crucified. The Last Supper was a celebration honoring both what Jesus had already done and what Jesus was about to do at Calvary. Read in Luke 22:19 where Luke gives a recount of that night's Communion and Jesus's final words:

> He took some bread and gave thanks to God for it. Then he broke it into pieces and gave it to the disciples, saying, "This is my body which is given for you. Do this to remember me."
>
> —NLT

Jesus told His disciples that it was the last time He would share a meal with them until His return. Communion is a reminder of what Jesus did at Calvary and a reminder that He will one day return for His bride, the church. Communion connects the old and the new, the past and the future, and it is a reminder of our soon coming reunion with Jesus Christ! I love the way the Message Bible states 1 Corinthians 11:26:

> What you must solemnly realize is that every time you eat this bread and every time you drink this cup, you reenact in your words and actions the death of the Master. You will be drawn back to this meal again and again until the Master returns. You must never let familiarity breed contempt.

LEAVE A LEGACY

I would be remiss if I didn't take so much of a brief minute to touch on the fact that your life, your memorials, your "it's not over" moments, both the victories and the pain, are combining piece by piece, forming your legacy. Your legacy is the information that will be passed from one generation to another, giving an exposé on your character and the choices you made. Who you are and the life you led will speak after you are gone. The decisions you make, the thoughts you think, and the actions you take are all being noted as a conglomerate story, soon to be called your legacy. This life is "but a fleeting moment," and the choices you make—the choice to not give up and to persist in the face of adversity—will outlive you. I'm sure you've heard the quote by Winston Churchill, "History will be kind to me, for I intend to write it."[2] All great men and women of character faced adversity and used the adversity to leave a lasting and powerful legacy. Anyone can sustain an easy life, but it takes character to finish the race with strength, commitment, and a pure heart before the Lord.

One of my wife's favorite poems, one she memorized in second grade, comes up often and during seasons of trial. A portion of the poem goes like this:

> When things go wrong, as they sometimes will,
> When the road you're trudging seems all uphill,
> When the funds are low and the debts are high,
> And you want to smile, but you have to sigh,
> When care is pressing you down a bit—
> Rest if you must, but don't you quit.
> Success is failure turned inside out
> The silver tint in the clouds of doubt,
> And you never can tell how close you are,
> It might be near when it seems afar;
> So stick to the fight when you're hardest hit—
> It's when things seem worst that you must not quit.[3]

Though I believe there are certain things that are important to quit, such as ungodly relationships, addictions, and sinful lifestyles, there are also things you shouldn't quit, especially and solely based on the presence of adversity. The time to quit is not during your trials. Don't quit your job, don't quit your marriage, don't quit on your kids, and don't quit on your pastor just because it is no longer easy.

When my son Josiah was born, Jennette and I knew the call of God was on his life, and so his name was chosen. For obvious reasons I love the story of the lasting and impactful legacy left by Josiah who took the throne at the age of eight.

Josiah faced adverse odds, went against popular opinion, and stood for what he knew to be right, despite the adverse consequences. King Josiah took the culture that his forefathers allowed to be infiltrated with rampant secularism and reclaimed the house of the Lord with worship. King Josiah was known to do what was right, despite the popular opinion of his day. (See 2 Kings 22:1–23:30; 2 Chronicles 34:1–35:27.)

Your legacy is not dependant on how old you are, what your family left you as an inheritance, or how many people are against you. Your legacy is determined by your obedience to the voice of God and the choices you make when you face those times when you have to hold onto everything you know and boldly believe that "it's not over."

10

I'M NOT OVER

"God has promised strength as our day, rest when we labor, light on the way, grace for our trials, help from above, unfading kindness, undying love."[1]

HOPE IF YOU'VE read this far with me, you've built your faith in knowing that God is on your side and wants to get involved in your circumstance. I believe that Josiah is a living, walking miracle today only by the grace of God. Because of His goodness my hope and desire is that you feel a renewal and sense of refreshed hope in God's covenant and promises with you. When God is involved in your situation, "it's not over"! I hope that this book has, in some small way, turned your heart into making this statement personal. Faith builds faith. When you read the victories of other people and see they are just like you and me, it builds your own faith.

There is a story you may remember in the news not too long about Jason McElwain, a high school student with autism. Jason served as one of the managers for his basketball team and became a favorite icon for not only the players but also for the fans with his often encouraging half-time pep talks. Jason loved basketball, but due to his illness, he and his parents never expected to him to *play* in a game. In the television spot that aired sharing Jason's story, the narrator says, "Who knew hope wore a blue shirt and black tie? Who knew hope spent hours shooting baskets in an empty gym? He worked all his life for a slim chance to play in just one game. Who knew hope would come off the bench with four minutes nineteen seconds to go?"[2] Yes, in the last game of the senior's season, Jason was called from the bench to experience what it felt like to play as an actual *player*. The stadium, his peers, and teammates went ecstatic. Hope was given a chance!

Jason's first shot was an air ball and missed the rim by a mile. There was desperation in the air as all eyes watched Jason experiencing a lifelong dream; he was actually playing in a basketball game after serving as the manager for the duration of his high school years. But playing in the game wasn't enough. Everyone wanted to see Jason make a least one basket. Another attempt and another miss. Time was running out. Jason was passed the ball for another chance, as he stood just outside the three-point circle. Amazingly, Jason shot and scored! The crowd went crazy. Basket after basket, Jason kept sinking three-point shots. In fact, Jason came out the high scorer that night with twenty points! Hope proved powerful in the life of an autistic high school senior.

Jennette and I love reading biographies of people who have

successfully made it through difficult and tough situations. I've asked a few friends to share their stories of victory, triumph, and faith. Some are very personal and real, and I salute their bravery for sharing with you and me. Read their journeys and be inspired to finish strong, and know when God is in it, there is no limit, and when God is in it, "it's not over."

TILL DEATH DO US PART

It was a beautiful summer morning, and I was sipping my tea and reading my Bible. What an amazing story when Jehoshaphat and his people won a great victory against three enemy armies that attacked them. How exciting. Such a victory. As I read, a verse jumped out at me, "You will not have to fight this battle. Take up your positions; stand firm and see the deliverance the LORD will give you, O Judah and Jerusalem. Do not be afraid; do not be discouraged. Go out to face them tomorrow, and the LORD will be with you" (2 Chron. 20:17, NIV).

I had a strong sense that this verse was for me. But I wasn't in a battle. Life was good. As pastors we were in a good place, having just bought a new church building. After twenty-six years of marriage we had a happy home, living life to the fullest with our four grown children. We even had a grandchild on the way. "No, Lord, we're not in a battle," I thought to myself. But I couldn't shake it. I had been warned; enemy forces were gathering, and this verse was going to be my lifeline.

Months passed, and I became increasingly uncomfortable with a friendship my husband was forming with a lady in our church. I confronted him, but he assured me it was innocent. I took him at his word against the intuition within me. I asked the Lord to show me what I needed to know. And He did. Just two weeks before Christmas I logged into our computer only to find his e-mail account open, and my world came crashing down. He was having an affair. Not a one-night stand. They had gone away on a weeklong vacation together.

It was over—our ministry, our marriage, our family. I confronted him, and I called my sister. I was leaving. I was done. I met with my two oldest daughters and told them what I had to do. Being at heart a godly man who spent his adult life devoted to his ministry and family, he begged me to stay and promised he would cut all ties with this woman. I agreed to allow our children to have Christmas as a family and then make the decision. We began to pick up the broken pieces, and the pain started to heal. But unbeknownst to me, the battle was still raging.

It became clear to me that my husband wanted his ministry, his children, his life—but not with me. That's a hard reality to deal with. I was devastated, and my instinct was to get as far away as I could. But that verse kept rising in my heart. I pictured Jehoshaphat in his battle. How impossible it must have looked. How terrifying to be surrounded on every side. Yet God gave him a strategy for victory.

I prayed, "Lord, I can see no way out of this but total ruin of our ministry and our family. But I want Your will for our lives. Give me the strategy to get through this, and I will do it."

You may wonder why I didn't just expose this sin and let others deal with it. I knew the sin had to be dealt with and that there would be consequences, but I needed to get God's mind on the whole situation first. I knew what people would advise me to do, but I had to hear it from Him. And I did. He repeatedly painted a picture of victory in my heart.

He led me strategically in three areas and kept reminding me, "Do not be afraid; do not be discouraged."

The emotions attached to betrayal can be overwhelming. Pain surges through your heart every moment of the day and snaps you awake in fear in the middle of the night. You can't sleep or eat. You feel a weight pressing down on you that makes you want to lie down and never get up again.

If I was going to do this God's way, then I had to stand back and realize that this was not about what an inadequate woman I was, nor was it about the younger, fun-loving other woman. This was a battle Satan was waging for my husband's life, our ministry, and our children's legacy. When I realized that, strength rose in my heart. I was not about to stand back and have the enemy decide our future. God had a plan for victory in a battle that only I seemed to see clearly. I had to shake off discouragement and replace my fears with faith. It was do or die.

Yet God said, "You will not have to fight this battle."

So what could I do? As I read on, I saw my part.

"Take up your positions; stand firm and see the deliverance the LORD will give you."

I know my position. In Christ I am more than a conqueror; I am well able. I can do all things through Him who strengthens me. So I took my position and stood firm on God's Word. I walked our house rebuking every demonic force that would try and stop God's plan for our lives. I boldly declared God's promises over our lives. That was my part, and God promised to do His part.

The second strategy the Lord gave me was to overwhelm my husband with love. I went out of my way to please him throughout the day and in the bedroom. I knew that if I withdrew from my husband sexually, I would be giving the devil the final foothold he needed. You may be thinking that is an act of desperation, but I knew that saving my family was worth it. The scripture kept coming to my mind, "A woman's family is held together by her wisdom, but it can be destroyed by her foolishness" (Prov. 14:1, CEV).

My husband had promised to stay away from the other woman even though he was struggling with his feelings, but he also felt so guilty and responsible for her that they stayed in contact. Only God kept him from walking out on me for good.

I made so many mistakes and faltered along the way. I lost my temper and did things out of desperation. There were many days when it looked like our marriage was over. One afternoon I came to the end of my rope and told him to leave, that I was just giving up. I was exhausted, finished. It was over. At that moment the phone rang. I answered it to hear the voice of a friend who knew nothing of our situation. She told me she was praying for me, and the Lord had told her to call and give me a word. She proceeded to prophesy that now was not the time to give up, that my prayers were working and victory was around the corner. She said I had a unique gift, and my place was significant alongside my husband. I laid my head on the kitchen counter and cried as she spoke. Once more God was telling me loudly and clearly, "It's not over!"

I knew that I had scriptural grounds on which to leave my marriage, and I knew that if my husband refused to repent completely, I would do it. I heard some wise advice that one should never get divorced because of emotions, rather to take time to deal with the anger and hurt before pulling the plug. That way you could look your children in the eye and say, "I did everything I could," and move on with no regrets.

I had been stopped from issuing an ultimatum on a number of occasions as the Lord directed me. In hindsight I think an ultimatum at the beginning of this saga would have short-circuited God's plan. Once I had done all I knew to do, I told my husband that I loved him with all my heart and honestly believed it was the will of God that brought us together. I then gave him a date that I would be announcing our separation and told him I had consulted a divorce lawyer even though it was not what I wanted.

The result was a total turnaround. My husband said he felt like a veil lifted off his eyes. He wept and repented, and we began to repair our marriage. He repented before the church, and we dealt with the consequences. We're so grateful that so many people have rallied around us and offered forgiveness.

This is a very personal story of our private pain, sin, and struggle. It's not easy to share, but we know something without any shadow of a doubt. When God says it's not over, it's not over!

—ANONYMOUS PASTOR'S WIFE

BUILT TO LAST

As the son of an Assemblies of God minister I grew up watching my dad pastor small churches across the East Coast and work as a residential builder on the side to take care of the financial needs of raising a family of six. My father taught me the trade and industry of construction, and we worked together until 1975 as a small building company. At that time my dad retired from building and pursued full-time ministry. With a family of my own, my wife, Sally, and I started our own construction company.

Our company grew and became very successful, but in 1987 the Lord started dealing with us to sell the company and make a drastic change in our lives. Both my wife and I had grown up in Christian homes, but we had a longing to experience God for ourselves. We both felt like God was asking us to make a change in our direction—a drastic change. We knew we were being called to leave everything behind and move to Oklahoma in order to attend a Bible training center to see for ourselves if all we had been taught as children was true. In May of 1988 we moved our family to Tulsa, Oklahoma, and in September we started attending school.

In order to facilitate this move and drastic change in our lives, my wife and I were able to solidify a buyer for our company and made an agreement with the new owners regarding our compensation. The new owners agreed to pay us monthly installments for the following five years. We thought we were financially set and had made fiscally responsible arrangements to cover our monthly needs while in school. But a turn of events left us in a so-called "wilderness experience" that truly tested our faith.

During the late 1980s the United States faced an economic crash when the government formed the Resolution Trust and radically altered the banking and finance industry. The results had a similar effect as that of our current economic situation. The new owners of our company were caught in this economic down-turn, and the results were a bankrupt company. After receiving our monthly installments for over a year, the money instantly dried up, and we were faced with no money and the decision whether we should stay in Bible school. But we knew in our hearts it wasn't over.

We believed that the answer was to continue the path we had started and finish school. Looking back, those were two of our best years and, yet, two of our toughest years at the same time. During those two years, we literally lost everything financially. We were so excited about what we were learning in school and how we were growing in God, but with two children the bills were quickly piling up. Sally and I both looked for jobs but couldn't seem to find one anywhere. We wondered what to do and were desperate for answers! We were nearing the end of our second year of school when the pastor of the church associated with our Bible school asked us to stay and build their new church facility. An answer to prayer—a job! It was to be a 250,000-square-foot church, which was the largest building we would have ever built up to that time. This was a huge blessing in our lives. But due to the collapse of our previous business, we still had multiple debts that continued to grow, until we were up to over $100,000 in credit card debt alone! We continued to believe it wasn't over.

After the completion of the building the pastor asked my wife and me to stay on salary and manage all of the facilities on the one-hundred-acre church campus, remodel the buildings, and run one of the largest ministry departments at the church. However, even with the salary we were making, there was no way outside of a miracle for us to even touch our mountain of debt. But it was a job, and we believed it was God opening a door. We decided to put our hope in the Lord and accepted the position.

Still swallowed by our sea of bills, we cried out to God for direction, and He showed us in the Bible where it says He would give seed to the sower. This was our answer! We had always paid our tithes and given offerings, but we knew this was God leading us to trust Him and give beyond what even seemed possible. With finances already tight, tithing was already a struggle. What difference would a little extra struggle be except an exercise for our faith? We decided to put God's Word to work and committed that the first $5,000 we could get our hands on, we would give it back to God as seed. In the natural this was one of the hardest things to do, because we desperately needed that money to put toward our debt. But we knew that if we *obeyed* God, He would see us though. It wasn't over!

We were obedient to sow that extra $5,000, and it wasn't long before we received a call from another pastor in our town. Their church had been hit by a tornado, and he said the Lord told him to call me to come manage the reconstruction of their church. I was excited and scared at the same time. I wasn't sure how my pastor, who was also my boss, would respond to the news that I wanted to moonlight on another job across town. I did not want to lose my steady income for this one project that would pay bills for a year or so but then leave me without a job again when the construction was complete.

I was sick thinking about what would happen, but in my heart I knew I was supposed to rebuild this other church. I finally got up the courage to talk to my pastor, and, only to the glory of God, he said he too believed I was supposed to build that church, and he said that they would keep me on salary and allow me to work on the other church while still maintaining my current duties on staff! That was the beginning of God moving our $100,000 mountain of debt before our very eyes. It wasn't over!

I began building the church across town, and, ironically, it just so happened that there were also some other buildings across the street that were also hit by the same tornado and was in need of repair. When they found out I was helping the neighboring church, they asked me to rebuild their buildings as well. Amazingly, building jobs continued over the next couple of years, and God kept providing seed in our hands. By this point we were able to put 100 percent of the construction profits toward our looming debt! By 2002 we not only had all of the credit cards paid off, but we also were able to pay off our house and cars as well! To this day we are completely debt free! It's still not over!

In the course of God paying off all of our debt, He was also setting us up to go into business full-time building churches all over the country! We now own *Churches by Daniels Construction*, and people all over the United States worship in buildings built by our company that started on nothing but faith and God's Word! We have seen the hand of God move in miraculous and mighty ways, and we firmly know that when you include God in the mix, no matter what it looks like, it's not over! All it takes is one word from God, and He can turn your situation around! No situation is too big for God. No matter what you are facing, you must know, it's never over! If it is His will for you to do it, He will make a way for it to happen!

—Charlie Daniels
Churches by Daniels Construction
Broken Arrow, OK

Breathe Again

Our family was in a season in our lives where we knew that we were in the center of God's will. Everything just seemed to be falling right into place, like no other time we remembered. A new job. A new city. A quick and profitable sale of our home. Finding the right new home. Expecting our third child, our first boy. It was going so well, and we were in a state of awe with all God was doing to us and through us. However, all the smiles would quickly fade and questions enter our minds in a matter of just a few hours.

Our family met for dinner, and my wife, Amanda, at seven and a half months pregnant, was feeling a lot of discomfort. While she tried to chalk it up to normal pregnancy discomfort, we both knew that something was happening. After talking with her doctor, we decided that a late night trip to the hospital would be best to put our minds at ease. Leaving the house, we never expected what was about to hit us.

Amanda began to experience intense labor pains. As the medical staff examined her, it became apparent to all that the baby was going to be born very soon. The doctors began to worry about Amanda's health and the health of the baby. Despite attempts to hold off delivery, at 6:43 a.m., Austin William Rearden entered this world via an emergency cesarean section, six weeks early.

As any parent can recall, the birth of a child is a joyous occasion. That was certainly the mood in the ER; however, it quickly changed when it was clear that Austin was having a very difficult time breathing. Being born early had not given Austin's lungs enough time to develop properly. I could see the concern on the faces of the nurses and doctors, which was confirmed as we quickly rushed from the ER to a place where we would become all to familiar, the neonatal intensive care unit.

A flood of emotions ran through my mind: Will he live? Will he be severely handicapped? What can I do to make this right? How did God allow this to happen? What are we going to do? All I could do was turn the situation over to God. Austin was in the care of the nurses and physicians trained to help him, but I knew he would need a touch from Almighty God.

I was quickly ushered out of the NICU so the medical staff could work without interference. All I could do was pray. Our son was lying in the hospital clinging to life, and it was totally and completely out of our hands. Nothing makes you feel more helpless and inadequate than when you are unable to help your children.

I left a baby in that room who was needing serious medical attention but otherwise appeared to be perfectly normal. He had a head full of hair, tiny feet and hands, baby soft skin, and features that proclaimed a perfect mix of mom and dad. I returned to a baby who was incubated, sedated, and monitored. He had been placed on a ventilator, many monitoring probes, and an arterial line to feed him. My heart was broken. While I had to be strong for my family, I would secretly slip away to cry, beg, and plead with God for my son's life.

We were still in the hospital over the Thanksgiving holiday, and though we had lots to be thankful for, we could not help but wonder what was going to happen to our new baby. He was on a ventilator, and we were holding out hope that his lungs would start to develop. Austin needed to be given several doses of surfactant to help this process along. We were starting to see some improvement as the initial doses were beginning to work.

Amanda was discharged from the hospital about four days after Austin was delivered. Nothing could prepare us for the emotions that we experienced as Amanda and

I drove away from the hospital with a car seat and no baby. We had to leave Austin in the NICU, still hooked up to all the machines and clinging to life. He was making progress, but we remained desperate for God to touch him. We would make the drive back and forth to the hospital many times over the next few weeks. A little over a week after Austin was born, Amanda was *finally* able to hold her son. He was still hooked up to monitors, but nothing compares to the feeling a mother has when she holds her baby for the very first time.

I remember one Sunday morning, I took my other two children to church and desperately prayed for Austin's healing. My specific prayer was that Austin would be strong enough to come off the ventilator, as that would be a big sign of his road to recovery. I desperately needed to see our family and friends at church, as they had been a constant support of love, encouragement, and prayer. But I would be lying if I told you that I was not crushed that Amanda and Austin were not with us in that service. I wanted my family to be together and completely whole. That morning our pastor preached a message about being an overcomer, and I latched onto that word for my son and my family. I was determined that no matter what the situation, we would continue to honor God because He is truly faithful and He has all of our lives in His control.

Following church I went to the hospital hoping for the best, but honestly expecting the status quo. I went through the normal routine of preparing to visit Austin, which included a thorough scrubbing of your hands and arms up to the elbows. As I was going through the scrubbing process, I noticed that the machines around Austin's bed were different from the ones that were there just hours earlier. I could also see the respiratory therapist working around him, and I just knew that God had answered our prayers. The ventilator had been removed, and Austin was making significant progress!

Austin continued on the road to recovery, and the feeding tube was finally removed. As the days passed by, Austin began to make a full recovery and was released from the hospital after several very long weeks in the NICU. Today he is a happy and perfectly healthy baby boy. He has suffered no ill effects from this rough start, and we know that God has a special plan for his life. Just when we were at the darkest hour of Austin's young life, we were made well aware that "it's not over."

—MATTHEW REARDEN
ORLANDO, FL

WHEN GOD IS IN IT

The Lord asked Sarah in Genesis 18:14, "Is anything too hard for the LORD?" Another scripture states, "For with God nothing will be impossible" (Luke 1:37). Whatever it is, He can and will do it if we put our trust in Him. Whether it be salvation, deliverance, healing, meeting financial needs—whatever it is, God is able.

What a wonderful surprise that after two boys God sent us a precious beautiful daughter, Julie Christina Meares. Two hours after Julie was born, the doctors awakened me in the wee hours of the morning to tell me that she had been placed in intensive care, possibly with pneumonia. From that time on it was a continuous battle with medical problems. Julie's blood count was abnormal, and her body lacked immunity.

When she was seven months old, Julie had a severe seizure brought on by an extremely high fever. We rushed her to the hospital where a concerned staff of doctors treated her and advised us to take her to her pediatrician in the morning. When we took our daughter to the doctor's office the next morning, we waited for what seemed like an eternity while he examined her. When he returned from the examination room, he told us that she had a severe heart murmur and that she should be taken to a heart specialist at Children's Hospital immediately.

We prayed, and I truly had peace that there was nothing wrong. The words that kept repeating over and over in my mind were, "The Lord will not give you more than you are able to bear." From that time on those words continued to be, and still are, implanted upon my heart.

After numerous X-rays and examinations, we were told that Julie needed surgery to correct some heart valves and possible small holes in her heart. Without surgery, the doctor cautioned, she would live only a few years, possibly three or four.

Little Julie sure needed something. She cried all the time. The doctor said this was due to the intense pain she was experiencing. The left side of her heart was the size of a three-year-old child's heart and caused tremendous pain for our little seven-month-old daughter.

After a three-month waiting period to enable Julie to gain weight and strength, she underwent successful surgery. But about seven days later, she began to dehydrate and was placed in isolation. After a while Julie seemed to rally and was able to come home. We thought all Julie's medical problems were solved and that we were back on the course to leading a normal life.

A few weeks later, however, she developed a fever of 109 degrees that lasted for over five hours with seizure after seizure following. The doctors and nurses were at a loss as what to do, and, as parents, we were puzzled as well. But then God let us hear His word again, "I will not let you experience more than you are able to bear." Julie's attacks were so severe that she had to be packed in ice when she stopped breathing many times and turned completely black from lack of oxygen. My husband, Virgil, stayed in the room holding Julie's hand and praying while the doctors and nurses were running back and forth with medications and oxygen. Julie's life was in the balance. Virgil spoke God's Word and prayed, "Lord, this child is in Your care. We have dedicated her to You, and she is Yours. We place her in Your arms." Julie's body began to relax, and she began breathing normally and slept a peaceful sleep for hours that night. Praise God!

Though we thought we had conquered Julie's health concerns, she still experienced problems with her health, some serious and some mild. Julie stopped breathing many times and was taken by ambulance to the hospital over and over during the next few years. Each time was a battle for her life. But the peace and victory came one night while Virgil and I were completely exhausted. We had been taking turns for months watching Julie to be sure that she would not smother herself or have another seizure during her sleep. One night I had a dream, and I heard God tell me these words while I slept, "Julie is healed. Not an instant healing, but a gradual healing. Peace, be still and sleep, for my angels are watching over her."

Praise the Lord! From that night on, my husband and I slept peacefully, with no fear that Julie would smother herself or have a seizure. Praise God for His grace and mercy.

God will meet you when you feel all is lost, when you feel that you can bear no more. He is there, not tired and worn out as we had become, but strong, alert, and waiting for us to say, "Lord, we need You, and we know by Your wonderful power that You are going to meet our need."

Julie is a living testimony that God heals. She graduated from college with two degrees in four years: one degree in international business and another degree in French with a minor in German. Julie speaks fluent French and German and has led teams on missions trips all over the world, including Africa, the Philippines, and other countries. Julie is able to say without a doubt, "God is a healer!"

—JANNIE MEARES
UPPER MARLBORO, MD

LOST BUT FOUND

I was married, and I had just had a brand-new baby. I had my college degree. I had a dream job, a beautiful home, and life seemed great! But in one moment it all changed. Unbeknownst to me my then husband was selling drugs out of our home. I had been home from the hospital three days with my precious baby girl when the police came and raided our house. They kicked the doors down. There were drug dogs, and they aimed a fleet of guns at us. It was a scene from a drug task force episode. My world was spinning, and in those few short moments I couldn't grasp what was happening to me. I threw my body on top of my infant baby and prayed to God that if the police fired their guns, the bullet would hit my body only and not my baby's.

As the daughter of a well-known pastor, my life was lived very publicly. As you can imagine, this story hit the nightly news, was all over the papers, and blasted on the Internet. It was horrific! Life as I knew it was over.

My then husband also decided that he no longer wanted to be married, so while awaiting trial, he moved back to his home state and began living a very single life-style. I was betrayed in the worst ways a woman can be, and I also had a legal issue pending that had potentially grave punishments.

My soul was broken. My heart felt as if it could no longer beat. I was mad at God. I felt betrayed by Him. I felt even God had left me. I pulled away and secluded myself into a darkness that cannot be described.

Though I was unaware of my husband's crimes, I stood before a judge with a possible life sentence for the many charges brought against my husband. I asked for mercy, and I had many letters written on my behalf from people who were willing to vouch for my actions and behaviors. Regardless, I felt it was over. Everything I thought I accomplished and loved vanished. I felt alone, betrayed, and lifeless. I stood there to be sentenced, with one parent on each side, numb, terrified, and hopeless. The judge ruled for probation and ordered a gigantic fine, along with a heavy load of community service hours. In that moment of escaping prison time, I couldn't see how God was holding me. I still felt my life was over and that it would never be the same.

I was right about one thing—my life would never be the same! It was soon to be better than before! One year after the sentencing and hearing, I realized I needed God. I decided to embark on a forty-day journey of fasting, prayer, writing, and seeking God. It started with these words, "Here I am, God; I need you!" I'll never forget the day I was driving in my car listening to the song "Moving Forward" (by Ricardo Sanchez and Israel Houghton). When I heard the lyrics, "You make all things new," something inside me broke and I began to weep. From that moment on God has restored back to me years that I lost. I love deeper, I sing louder, I pray harder, and I celebrate waking up. I celebrate life. I am on a mission to destroy the devil and share my story. Although there are so many other layers, details, twists, and turns to my story, the message remains the same: even when I couldn't pray, even when I couldn't see a future, even when I couldn't sing, even when I felt no hope, God was there with me. He was writing my story.

I am now remarried to a worship pastor. He is amazing and represents restoration. He is my true love, and I would go through this all over again to find myself carrying his last name! He is my strength, my godly counsel, and he embodies what a godly husband is. I never knew the life that was waiting for me on the other side of this trial. I should be dead. I should be in prison. The world says I should be a lot of things, But God says I am His child. God says, "It's not over for you, Nicole." There are truly no limits when God is carrying you. The darkest, most devastating hurt and pain, the most lonely, lifeless season I was in, was truly what I believed was my end. But my setbacks only propelled me into my comeback.

I am in eternal love with the Most High. He is the lover of my soul and the reason I sing. He is the reason I live and the force that drives me. Do not let go. Hold on! The darkness has to come before the morning, but the morning is coming. God is faithful. And when He restores, it doesn't go back to the good place you were in. God makes it better than before. Don't quit. What if today is the day your breakthrough comes!

—Nicole Richey
Decatur, AL

When Suddenly Happens

The day started out normal. Justin, who was two at the time, went to school and came back feeling fine and then lay down for a nap. Jay, my husband, and our older two boys, Josh and Jace, were out of town at a tractor show in South Florida with my dad.

Justin had slept for a really long time this particular Wednesday, and I had checked on him several times. Justin had no fever and was sleeping well, but when he had been asleep for almost six hours, I knew that something was not right. When I woke him up, he was not able to stand well. He would walk kind of sideways as if he had vertigo. He was just whimpering and looking through me. You could tell there was something going on, but it was hard to pinpoint any immediate triggers. I reached in and got him out of his crib. Immediately Justin started throwing up—a lot.

As I attempted to place him on the ground and in the light, it was obvious he wasn't able to stand at all. As I spoke to him, it became very clear that his speech was not normal based upon his usual habits. Through trembling, I called the doctor and got in touch with the triage nurse who asked me, "How fast can you drive him to Scottish Rite Hospital?" My heart sank. Scottish Rite is known to be one of the best children's hospitals in the country, but we live about one and a half hours away. Without hesitation I told her that I was on my way. Justin was still throwing up, but I put him in his car seat, and we took off. I was praying as I drove. I knew something was seriously wrong with my baby. I began to cry out to God. Praying, crying, praying. When we approached the city limits, I felt hope was in sight. But Justin went unconscious still about thirty miles away from the hospital. Though we weren't at Scottish Rite, we happened to be next to another hospital, and I rushed Justin into the emergency room.

When I walked in with Justin, the ER was overcrowded. There was no place to sit or even stand, but they took us immediately back to see a doctor. Justin was whisked away for a CT scan of his brain. I had no idea what was going on. The doctors and nurses began to act with an intense urgency, but they still hadn't given me any indication what was going on with Justin. They were rushing and bustling. They called an ambulance to come and get him, and off we went to Scottish Rite.

At this point I still had no idea what was going on. I knew that it was not something normal, but there was a steady peace that ran through my spirit. I was concerned but had a serene calm in my heart. It was almost not even real. I sat there watching doctors and nurses buzz to and fro. I was there, but I was unaware and aware all at the same time. By this time we had arrived at Scottish Rite, and there were doctors buzzing about, and we were actually moved very quickly from the ER to a room—a room in which we lived in for a total of a month. Doctors had no idea what was going on with Justin. They thought at first that he had been poisoned, but blood tests ruled that out immediately. Then they thought it was meningitis.

No one really could identify anything specific in regard to Justin's condition. They ran all kinds of tests—spinal taps, twenty-four-hour urine catches, MRIs, lots of blood work, and other physical tests. His condition was getting worse. He was not able to hold things. He seemed to be having nonstop, palsy-type jerking movements in one hand. The other hand was not as usable. His face was drawn, and he did not seem to know much about his surroundings.

By this time my husband was at the hospital with me, and we both felt it necessary to continue to praise God even though we didn't understand what was going on. We weren't praising God because Justin was sick; we were praising God because we knew, no matter what was causing this ailment, God was Justin's healer. Finally we were told that Justin had a brain tumor and that he would not be going home with us for quite some time. The doctors told my husband and me that Justin was in very, very progressed stage of illness, and this was going to be the end for our youngest son.

Prayers were covering Justin and our family from every direction. We had church pastors and staff praying over Justin. We had friends and family praying. People from other churches and other states were praying for Justin. Pastors from other communities were coming to pray and stand with us during this trial.

Despite the dismal report the doctors repeatedly told us, my husband I continued to speak life over Justin's body. The medical staff even sent grief counselors to help my husband and me deal and cope with the reality they thought we were avoiding.

Then one *amazing* day, out of the blue, Justin stood on his own and shocked the doctors. Though Justin's steps were feeble and wobbly, I was shouting and running to get everyone's attention. This was major progress for

Justin. Then, little by little, Justin began to regain strength, mobility, and the use of his extremities.

After several months of physical therapy, occupational therapy, and speech therapy, the Lord restored Justin above and beyond. To this day the doctors are unable to provide an explanation for what happened to Justin. To God be the everlasting glory! Justin is now at home, running, playing, and giggling with his two older brothers, his dad, and me. So, yes, I can say with absolute confidence, our God is good!

—Melissa Reeder
Gainesville, GA

NOTES

Chapter 1
The Pressing of Life

1. "I Need Thee Every Hour" by Annie S. Hawks. Public domain.
2. Richard Gray, "Grief Leaves the Body at Risk of Infection," *The Telegraph*, March 25, 2012, http://www.telegraph.co.uk/health/healthnews/9164466/Grief-leaves-the-body-at-risk-of-infection.html (accessed May 22, 2012).

Chapter 2
The Waiting Room of Life

1. "When the Waiting Time" by Fred A. Fillmore. Public domain.
2. Patricia Datchuck Sánchez, "Waiting and Welcoming the Coming One," Celebration Publications, http://www.nationalcatholicreporter.org/sanchez/locked/cyclea/adventa/advent295a.htm (accessed June 12, 2012).
3. Rick Warren, *The Purpose Driven Church: Growth Without Compromising Your Message and Mission* (Grand Rapids, MI: Zondervan, 1996), 393-394.

CHAPTER 3
THE STRENGTH OF STRUGGLE

1. "Amazing Grace" by John Newton. Public domain.
2. WikiAnswers, "What Was the Average Age of the Twelve Disciples When They Joined Jesus?", http://wiki.answers.com/Q/What_was_the_average_age_of_the_twelve_disciples_when_they_joined_Jesus (accessed June 12, 2012); The Happy Surprise, "Jesus' Disciples: A Teenage Posse?", http://kbonikowsky.wordpress.com/2008/08/20/jesus-disciples-a-teenage-posse/ (accessed June 12, 2012).
3. Guardian.co.uk, "50 Stunning Olympic Moments No3: Derek Redmond and Dad Finish 400m," http://www.guardian.co.uk/sport/blog/2011/nov/30/50-stunning-olympic-moments-derek-redmond (accessed June 12, 2012).

CHAPTER 4
THE VALLEY OF WHY

1. "Where He Leads I'll Follow" by W. A. Ogden. Public domain.
2. Bible-Library.com, s.v. "dothan," http://bible-library.com/Dothan (accessed June 12, 2012).

CHAPTER 5
THE "NOT" SPOT

1. "Breathe on Me, Breath of God" by Edwin Hatch. Public domain.

2. TruthBook.com, "Does God Exist," http://
www.truthbook.com/stories/dsp_viewStory
.cfm?storyID=487 (accessed June 12, 2012).

3. TheFreeDictionary.com, s.v. "bitter," http://www
.thefreedictionary.com/bitter (accessed May 23, 2012).

4. "I Am Forgiven" by Israel Houghton and Ricardo
Sanchez. Copyright © 2009. Integrity's Hosanna!
Music, Integrity's Praise! Music, New Breed
Extended, RicardoMusic.com, Sound Of The New
Breed. Administered by EMI Christian Music Pub-
lishing. Permission requested.

5. ABCNews.go.com, "Do Men or Women Worry
More?", *Good Morning America*, http://abcnews
.go.com/GMA/Health/story?id=1653218#
.Tua5kZgrWp0%20–%20worry%20stats (accessed
June 12, 2012).

6. Paul Revoir, "We Worry for Two Hours a Day
Because of the Credit Crunch," *Daily Mail*, http://
www.dailymail.co.uk/news/article-1102866/We
-worry-hours-day-credit-crunch.html (accessed June
12, 2012).

CHAPTER 6
BEAUTY FOR ASHES—THE EXCHANGE

1. "What Would You Give in Exchange?" by F. J. Berry.
Public domain.

2. "It's Not Over" by Israel Houghton and Ricardo Sanchez. Copyright © 2011. Integrity's Praise! Music,

Sound Of The New Breed, RicardoMusic.com. Permission requested.

3. Kevin Conner and Ken Malmin, *The Covenants* (Portland, OR: City Bible Publishing, 1997).

4. "All Praise to Thee, Eternal Lord" by Martin Luther. Public domain.

5. "Help Us, O Jesus, Thou Mighty Defender" by Johann H. Schröder. Public domain.

6. Mike Hullah, "Covenant—The Basis of Biblical Relationships," SermonCentral.com, http://www.sermoncentral.com/sermons/covenant--the-basis-of-biblical-relationships-mike-hullah-sermon-on-unity-65343.asp?page=2 (accessed June 12, 2012).

7. "Christians and Their Covenant Relationship With God" sermon preached at Grace Baptist Fellowship, http://www.traviscase.org/Sermons/Covenants/CovenantRelationship.html (accessed June 12, 2012).

CHAPTER 7
THE PILLARS OF HOPE

1. "My Hope Is Built on Nothing Less" by Edward Mote. Public domain.

2. Dictionary.com, s.v. "hope," http://dictionary.reference.com/browse/hope (accessed May 24, 2012).

3. *The American Heritage Dictionary of the English Language, Fourth Edition* (Boston: Houghton Mifflin Company, 2006), s.v. "hope."

4. Jerome Groopman, *The Anatomy of Hope* (New York: Random House Publishers, Inc., 2005).

5. Cancer Wellness Center, "Hope, Statistics and the Will to Live," http://www.cancerwellnesscenter.org/ HopeandtheWilltoLive.html (accessed June 12, 2012).

6. Paul Rousseau, "Hope in the Terminally Ill," PMC US National Library of Medicine National Institutes of Health, http://www.ncbi.nlm.nih.gov/pmc/articles/ PMC1071019/ (accessed June 12, 2012).

7. J. R. Averill, G. Catlin, and K. K. Chon, *Rules of Hope* (New York: Springer-Verlag, 1990).

CHAPTER 8
DON'T WAIT TO CELEBRATE

1. "Bless the Lord, O My Soul." Public domain.

2. Wisegeek.com, "What Is a Sound Wave?", http:// www.wisegeek.com/what-is-a-sound-wave.htm (accessed June 12, 2012).

3. "I'm Not Ashamed" by Israel Houghton and Ricardo Sanchez. Copyright © 2009. Integrity's Hosanna! Music, Integrity's Praise! Music, New Breed Extended, Ricardo Music.com, Sound Of The New Breed. Permission requested.

CHAPTER 9
DON'T FORGET TO REMEMBER

1. "Revive Us Again" by William P. MacKay. Public domain.

2. Thinkexist.com, "Winston Churchill Quotes," http://thinkexist.com/quotation/

history_will_be_kind_to_me_for_i_intend_to_
write/191686.html (accessed May 25, 2012).

3. "Don't Quit" author unknown. Public domain.

CHAPTER 10
I'M NOT OVER

1. "God's Promise," by Sel. by Eld. T. H. Crawford. Public domain.

2. ABC, The Finals, http://www.youtube.com/ watch?v=r93vABC1M7A (accessed June 12, 2012).

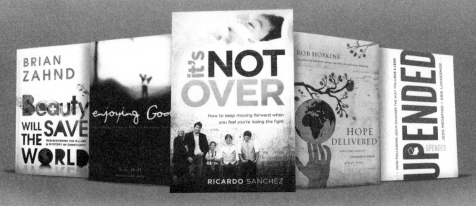